THE MACMILLAN COMPANY
NEW YORK · BOSTON · CHICAGO · DALLAS
ATLANTA · SAN FRANCISCO

MACMILLAN & CO., LIMITED
LONDON · BOMBAY · CALCUTTA
MELBOURNE

THE MACMILLAN CO. OF CANADA, LTD.
TORONTO

STARVED ROCK

BY

EDGAR LEE MASTERS

Author of "Spoon River Anthology," "Songs and
Satires," "The Great Valley," "Toward
the Gulf," etc.

New York
THE MACMILLAN COMPANY
1919

Certain of these poems first appeared in *Reedy's Mirror*, *Poetry*, *The Cosmopolitan*, *The Yale Review* and *The New York Sun*.

Of kindred things: as an oak whose leaves are sere
Fly over the valley when the winds are keen,
And nestle where the earth receives
Another generation of exhausted leaves.

* * * * *

Fatigued with age its sleepless eyes look over
Fenced fields of corn and wheat,
Barley and clover.
The lowered pulses of the river beat
Invisibly by shores that stray
In progress and retreat
Past Utica and Ottawa,
And past the meadow where the Illini
Shouted and danced under the autumn moon,
When toddlers and papooses gave a cry,
And dogs were barking for the boon
Of the hunter home again to clamorous tents
Smoking beneath the evening's copper sky.
Later the remnant of the Illini
Climbed up this Rock, to die
Of hunger, thirst, or down its sheer ascents
Rushed on the spears of Pottawatomies,
And found the peace
Where thirst and hunger are unknown.

* * * * *

This is the tragic and the fateful stone
Le Rocher or Starved Rock,
A symbol and a paradigm,
A sphinx of elegy and battle hymn,

[2]

STARVED ROCK

As a soul from whom companionships subside
The meaningless and onsweeping tide
Of the river hastening, as it would disown
Old ways and places, left this stone
Of sand above the valley, to look down
Miles of the valley, hamlet, village, town.

  *   *   *   *   *

It is a head-gear of a chief whose head,
Down from the implacable brow,
Waiting is held below
The waters, feather decked
With blossoms blue and red,
With ferns and vines;
Hiding beneath the waters, head erect,
His savage eyes and treacherous designs.

  *   *   *   *   *

It is a musing memory and memorial
Of geologic ages
Before the floods began to fall;
The cenotaph of sorrows, pilgrimages
Of Marquette and LaSalle.
The eagles and the Indians left it here
In solitude, blown clean

[1]

CONTENTS

CONTENTS

[vii]

STARVED ROCK

Whose lips unlock
Life's secret, which is vanishment, defeat,
In epic dirges for the races
That pass and leave no traces
Before new generations driven in the blast
Of Time and Nature blowing round its head.
Renewing in the Present what the Past
Knew wholly, or in part, so to repeat
Warfare, extermination, old things dead
But brought to life again
In Life's immortal pain.

     *   *   *   *   *

What Destinies confer,
And laughing mock
LaSalle, his dreamings stir
To wander here, depart
The fortress of Creve Coeur,
Of broken heart,
For this fort of Starved Rock?
After the heart is broken then the cliff
Where vultures flock;
And where below its steeps the savage skiff
Cuts with a pitiless knife the rope let down
For water. From the earth this Indian town
Vanished and on this Rock the Illini
Thirsting, their buckets taken with the knife,
Lay down to die.

     *   *   *   *   *

STARVED ROCK

This is the land where every generation
Lets down its buckets for the water of Life.
We are the children and the epigone
Of the Illini, the vanished nation.
And this starved scarp of stone
Is now the emblem of our tribulation,
The inverted cup of our insatiable thirst,
The Illini by fate accursed,
This land lost to the Pottawatomies,
They lost the land to us,
Who baffled and idolatrous,
And thirsting, spurred by hope
Kneel upon aching knees,
And with our eager hands draw up the bucketless rope.

*   *   *   *   *

This is the tragic, the symbolic face,
Le Rocher or Starved Rock,
Round which the eternal turtles drink and swim
And serpents green and strange,
As race comes after race,
War after war.
This is the sphinx whose Memnon lips breathe dirges
To empire's wayward star,
And over the race's restless urges,
Whose lips unlock
Life's secret which is vanishment and change.

HYMN TO THE DEAD

O, you who have gone from the ways of cities,
From the peopled places, the streets of strife,
From offices, markets, rooms, retreats,
Pastoral ways, hamlets, everywhere from the earth,
And have made of the emptiness of your departure
A land, a country, a realm all your own,
Set above the hills of our vision, an empire
Within, around, above our empire of days,
Of pain and clamorous tongues;
An empire which out of a sovereign silence
Stretches its power over the restless multitude
Of our thoughts, and the ceaseless music of our beings,
And surrounds us even as the air we breathe —
O ye majestic Dead, hear our hymn!

*   *   *   *   *

The clown, the wastrel and the fool in life
Are lifted up by you, O Death!
The least of these who has entered in
Your realm, O Death,
Is greater than the greatest of us,
And by a transfiguration has been clothed
With the glory and the wonder of nature.
He has drunk of the purple cup of apotheosis,
And passed through the mystical change,

[5]

And accomplished the cycle of being.
He has risen from the lowlands of earth
Into the air on wings of breath.
He has rejected the shell of the body, feet and hands,
He has become one with the majesty of Time,
And taken the kingdom of triumph
Whether it be cessation or bliss.
For he has entered into the kingdom of primal powers,
Being or ceasing to be,
Even as he has re-entered the womb of nature.
Or he has found peace,
States of wisdom, or vision —
Hail! realm of Silence,
Whence comes the unheard symphony too deep for
    strings,
Hail, infinite Light,
Darkness to eyes of flesh —
All hail!

*   *   *   *   *

What are we, the living, beside you the dead?
We of daily hunger, daily food, daily ablutions,
The daily rising and lying down,
Waking and sleep;
The daily care of the body's needs;
And daily desire to pass the gift of life;
And daily fears of the morrow to come;
And daily pains for things that are gone;
And daily longing for things that fly us;
And sorrow that follows wherever we go;

[6]

HYMN TO THE DEAD

And love that mocks us, and peace that breaks,
And shame that tracks us, and want that gnaws.
But O ye Dead! Ye great ones,
Triumphant over these, released
From the duties of dust, all chains of desire,
And made inhabitants of breathless spaces,
Immanent in a realm of calm,
Rulers of a sphere of tideless air,
Victors returned from the war of death in life,
Victors over death in death!

*   *   *   *   *

For the growing soul turns in
Even as the seed turns in on itself,
And becomes hard, transparent,
An encased life, condensed
In the process of saving itself
From rains that beat in the fall,
And frosts that descend from skies grown cold.
And we who shed away old thoughts and hopes,
Days and dreams of life
Turn in, grow clear like grains of rice,
Until the realm of death
Is as snow delivered land
Luring the seed —
And it becomes our home, our country,
Our native land that calls us back
From this sojourn of adventure,
And place of profit;
For O ye majestic Dead, your absence draws us,

[7]

STARVED ROCK

If it be naught but absence still you summon,
Your absence has become a very Presence,
A Power, a hierarchy of Life!

*　　　*　　　*　　　*　　　*

Even as leaves enrich the earth
Layer on layer,
Even as bodies of men enrich the soil
Generation on generation,
So do the spirits of those departed
Enrich our soil of life
With delights, wisdoms, purest hopes,
And shapes of beauty.
But oh beyond all these, is our life enriched
With exalted contemplations
Of you, O glorious Dead,
Who have eaten of the tree of life and become gods,
Friendly divinities to us who remain,
Dear familiars, as you were with us
Fathers, children, lovers, friends.
Ye who sense with the inner eye,
Since nothing in our days of living
Moves uncolored of your splendors,
Presences to which all things relate!

*　　　*　　　*　　　*　　　*

O realm of the Dead,
Black Mountain, if you be,
Which darkens heaven,
And shadows earth,
Round which our spirits flutter

HYMN TO THE DEAD

Like startled moths.
Black mountain with whose blackness
The light of life is mixed,
Whereof all hues are made:
All thoughts, all lofty wanderings of the soul,
All meanings, divinations
Of briefest hours, and frailest joys,
All wonders of the spectrum of the soul
Out of life and death!

*   *   *   *   *

Realm of the Dead!   Supreme Reality
All Hail!

CREATION

Passion flower unfolding in darkness!
Glow-worm under a spray of lilac!
Flame on the altar of love!
Beloved in your chamber!
The phoenix moon rising from the ashes of day
Spreads her wings of saffron fire
Above the enchanted garden.
And I brush away the leaves of night
To find the star of my love.
I part the curtains about the altar,
I enter your chamber, beloved.

*   *   *   *   *

I have entered your chamber, beloved,
I have found my star.
Between kisses and whispers
And the silken touch of flesh
Breast to breast, lips to lips,
Our souls are seeking and drifting!
As an albatross hovers and flies
With the running sea . . .
Powers of body, powers of spirit,
Divinities
Awakened never before,
Hidden in nerves asleep, in veins without a tide

CREATION

Flow through us.
I give you my life, beloved,
For life of you, given to me —
O bride of love!

*   *   *   *   *

O hair of fire! O breasts of light,
Like double stars!
O voice like a lute that whispers
At midnight, in a bower of roses!
O body luminous as the nebulous waste
Across the midnight,
Pour on my breast, my hands, my brow
The sacred fire,
As our flesh becomes one
Upborne by your breasts,
White as bridal blossoms
Where there is yet no milk,
But only eddying blood
Circling in whirlpools of delirious ecstasy
In time with the blood of me.
Our lips together, our bodies together
While the yearning urn of porphyry
Waits to drink the silver stream,
And thirsts to drink,
And poises like a gold fish waiting
For the stream of silver fire. . . .

But oh, hands of me that clasp your sunny head,
Drawing it close to my breast,

[11]

STARVED ROCK

In rapture of its beauty!
O temple of your spirit!
Spirit of you which I woo and would win,
In rapture without will,
In rapture blind, save for the inspired urge,
In rapture seeking further rapture,
In rapture to wed your spirit fully,
And all your spirit, which my spirit
Through the unity of flesh would reach
And win, and keep —
Bride of lightning!
Bride of Life!

      *   *   *   *   *

As when the butterfly slowly moves his wings
Drawing from the virgin core of honeysuckles
The sweetest drop of dew: —
So pause his wings spread wide
When all is gained.

      *   *   *   *   *

Goddess of the white dawn,
Let my beloved sleep —
Robins that sing at dawn,
Wake not my beloved!
I sleep with my beloved,
And she sleeps with me,
And a life sleeps now
That will wake!

THE WORLD'S DESIRE

At Philae, in the temple of Isis,
The fruitful and terrible goddess,
Under a running panel of the sacred ibis,
Is pictured the dead body of Osiris
Waiting the resurrection morn.
And a priest is pouring water blue as iris
Out of a pitcher on the stalk of corn
That from the body of the god is growing,
Before the rising tides of the Nile are flowing.
And over the pictured body is this inscription
In the temple of Isis, the Egyptian:
This is the nameless one, whom Isis decrees
Not to be named, the god of life and yearning,
Osiris of the mysteries,
Who springs from the waters ever returning.

At the gate of the Lord's house,
Ezekiel, the prophet, beheld the abomination of Babylon:
Women with sorrow on their brows
In lamentation, weeping
For the bereavement of Ishtar and for Tammuz sleeping,
And for the summer gone.
Tammuz has passed below
To the house of darkness and woe,

STARVED ROCK

Where dust lies on the bolt and on the floor
Behind the winter's iron door;
And Ishtar has followed him,
Leaving the meadows gray, the orchards dim
With driving rain and mist,
And winds that mourn.
Ishtar has vanished, and all life has ceased;
No flower blossoms and no child is born.

But not as Mary Magdalen came to the tomb,
The women in the gardens of Adonis,
Crying, " The winter sun is yet upon us,"
Planted in baskets seeds of various bloom,
Which sprouted like frail hopes, then wilted down
For the baskets' shallow soil.
Then for a beauty dead, a futile toil,
For leaves that withered, yellow and brown,
From the gardens of Adonis into the sea,
They cast the baskets of their hope away:
A ritual of the things that cease to be,
Brief loveliness and swift decay.

And O ye holy women, who at Delphi
Roused from sleep the cradled Dionysius,
Who with an April eye
Looked up at them,
Before the adorable god, the infant Jesus,
Was found at Bethlehem!

For at Bethlehem the groaning world's desire
For spring, that burned from Egypt up to Tyre,

And from Tyre to Athens beheld an epiphany of fire:
The flesh fade flower-like while the soul kept breath
Beyond the body's death,
Even as nature which revives;
In consummation of the faith
That Tammuz, the Soul, survives,
And is not sacrificed
In the darkness where the dust
Lies on the bolt and on the floor,
And passes not behind the iron door
Save it be followed by the lover Christ,
The Ishtar of the faithful trust,
Who knocks and says: "This soul, which winter knew
In life, in death at last,
Finds spring through me, and waters fresh and blue.
For lo, the winter is past;
The rain is over and gone.
I open! It is dawn!"

TYRANNOSAURUS: OR BURNING
LETTERS

Trees of the forest ground to pulp,
Rolled into sheets and rabbit tracked
With nut-gall or with nigrosine —
Then look at spirits thrill, or gulp
A lost delight, a rising spleen
For love that grew intense or slacked . . .

Here are the letters, torn in bits,
Crammed in the basket, look how full!
Our little fireplace scarce admits
So much that once was beautiful.
Here where we sat and dreamed together
In March, and now when we should be
Friends in the glory of June weather,
We tear our letters up — oh, me!
Call Jane to take the basket down,
And throw these on the furnace fire.
Let ashes drift about the town
Of what was our desire!

What are we to the gods, I wonder?
Perhaps two crickets in the grass,
Who meet and drop their stomachs' plunder
To touch antennæ as they pass.

TYRANNOSAURUS

So kissing in such soul communion
The gardener's step is heard, and quick
The crickets break their spirits' union,
Hide under logs or bits of brick.
Does guilty conscience stir the crickets?
What does he care? Why not a snap.
He's trimming out the hazel thickets
For a tennis court and shooting trap. . . .
You are afraid of God! Not that?
Some step has frightened you, I know.
Well, then it's gossip the alley-cat.
At least our hands grow cold as snow,
Relax their touch, and then we come,
Tear up the letters, sit and stare
Some moments, wholly dumb!

If we are crickets, still our breasts
Contain for us things real enough.
The gods may laugh, their interests
Are what? I wonder — not the love
Such as we knew. To be a god
Through love is what I hoped, and rise
Above the level of the clod.
They said it can't be, who are wise,
That's not the way to win the prize:
Or if it be, I don't know how;
Or you are not the one with whom
I might have won it. Well, my brow
Is turned into a whitened tomb
With all uncleanness in it; dreams

STARVED ROCK

Rotting away with hopes as fair . . .
To me, the liver, nothing seems
Won that is lost. I can't invert,
Sophisticate the facts, or swear
My evil good. A hurt's a hurt,
A loss a loss, a scar a scar,
A spirit frustrate is inert.
To stretch your hands toward a star
And lose the star, or have it die
To ashes like a rocket, alters
The aspect of your being's sky.
You've learned no praise from earthly psalters
Can win the star, or else you've learned
The star you touched was quickly turned
To ashes while it burned.

Hell! Let us face it. Here it is
We had some walks, some precious talks,
Some hours of paradise and bliss.
Our blossom opened, we inhaled
All of its fragrance, now I scowl
Because our wonder blossom paled
For lack of water in the bowl
Tipped over by the alley-cat,
Or what not, change, distrust or fear;
Your pride, your will, a hovering gnat
I struck at striking you, a blear
Of eyes a moment, making blind
My vision, yours. . . . Or there's the age,
The age is frightful to my mind,

TYRANNOSAURUS

Nothing to do but stand it — well
I sit here and say " hell."

For it's really hell to have a will,
It's hell to hope and to believe,
That good can swallow up the ill,
That gods are working, will achieve.
They may be, yet they disregard
Our cricket feelings, so we shrill
Sonnets and elegies round the yard . . .
Let's talk a bit of chlorophyll:
The sun was useless for our life,
No wine, no beef, no watercress
Until this chlorophyll grew rife
Millions of years since, more or less.
And if no wine or beef, no love,
No pulp, no paper, nigrosine,
No letters which are made thereof.
Think! All we found and lost has been
Through chlorophyll.

                    And just suppose
Nature should lose the secret power
For making chlorophyll, the rose
We cherished would not come to flower.
No other man and woman more
Would burn their letters grieving — yet
We may be rising, for who knows
There may be something vastly better
Than love to flame and flay and fret,

And hate this letter and that letter,
Once rid of chlorophyll, in case
A subtler substance could be given
To this poor globe out of heaven —
We are a weak, if growing race!

Here, then, I think is a moral for us,
Another is tyrannosaurus —
Tyrannosaurus, what of him,
The monarch of this world one time,
Back in the æons wet and dim?
He faded like a pantomime.
And he could, well, step over trees,
Crunch up bowlders like cracking nuts,
Flip horses away like bumble-bees,
Stretch out in valleys as if they were ruts;
And hide a man in his nostril's hole,
And crush young forestry just like weeds.
He came and went, and what's your soul,
And what is mine with their crying needs?
And love that seemed eternal once,
Given of God to lift, inspire,
Well — now do we see? Was I dunce
Drunk with the wine of soul's desire?
Who made that wine, why did I drink it?
Why did I want it? What's the game?
Are spirits chaos? I scarce can think it.
Why fly for the light and get the flame?
Is love for souls of us chlorophyll
That makes us eatable, sweet and crisp

TYRANNOSAURUS

For Gods that raise us to feed their fill?
Who lives, the dreamer, the will o' the wisp?
Do Gods live, vanish, return again?
Who in the devil has love or luck?
One thing is true, there's rapture and pain.
As for the rest, I pass the buck.
Something occurs, and God knows what,
Tyrannosaurus fades like a ghost.
That throws a light on our little lot,
Love that is won, love that is lost.
Even a hundred years from now,
If this poor earth is rolling still,
Hearts will quiver, break or bow —
Provided the plants have chlorophyll.

Oh well! Oh hell! We must be heroic,
And it helps to scan a million of years.
And to think of monstrous beasts mesoic,
Brightens, though it dries no tears.
I'll dream for life of our walks by the river —
That was March and it's now July.
And this remains: I'll love you forever —
Burn up the letters now — Good by!

LORD BYRON TO DOCTOR POLIDORI

No more of searching, Doctor — let it go.
It can't be lost. I have a memory
I put it in a drawer, or again
I seem to see me tuck it in a pocket
Of some portmanteau. If you find the letter
Deliver it to Moore. But if it's lost,
The story is not lost. I tell you this
To save the story from my side. Attend!
It was this way:

                              Allegra had become
A child requiring care, and nutritive
Instruction in religion, morals, well,
They call me blasphemer and sensualist,
But read my poems. Christianity
Was never of rejected things with me.
The Decalogue is good enough, I think.
And Shelley's theories, atheist speculations
I never shared — nor social dreams. The scheme
Of having all things, women, too, in common
Means common women. I have sinned, I know —
I call it sin. The marriage vow I honor,
And woman's virtue. Though I stray, I hold
That women should be chaste, though man is not.
That's why I placed Allegra in a convent. . . .

LORD BYRON TO DOCTOR POLIDORI

Now to the letter, and my story of it.

The mother, Claire, Claire Claremont, as you know —
Pined for Allegra; would possess the child
And take her from the convent — where?   No doubt
To Shelley's nest, where William Godwin's daughter
Raised on free love, and Shelley preaching it,
And Claire in whom 'tis bred, hold sway, who read,
Talk, argue, dream of freedom, all the things
Opposed to what is in the present order.
You know the notes to "Queen Mab."   Well, I say
This suits me not.

           So Shelley and his wife,
Mary, the planet of an hour, since quenched,
Conceive I keep Allegra where she is
From wounded pride, or pique.   Hell fire!   They think
I'm hurt for thinking Claire and Shelley join
Their lips in love, and masque my jealousy
By just this pose of morals, make reprisal
Under a lying flag, and keep Allegra
To punish Claire and sate my jealousy
By this hypocrisy — It makes me laugh.

But to pursue.   A maid who was discharged
From Shelley's household told the credible tale
That Claire was Shelley's mistress, and the Hoppners
Heard and believed — why not?   As she is fair,
And Shelley wrote "Love is like understanding
Which brighter grows gazing on many truths,

[23]

Increases by division," that himself
Could not accept the code, a man should choose
One woman and leave all the rest, why not?
As for myself, I have not preached this doctrine,
Though living it as men do in the world. . . .

Oh yes, I know this love called spiritual,
Of which old maids, whose milk has gone to brain
And curdled in the process, and who hate me
For taking men and women as they are,
Talk to create belief for self and others.

Denial makes philosophies, religions.
Indulgence leaves one sane, objectifies
The eternal womanly, freeing brain of fumes,
To work with master hands with love and life.

The story rose, however.

                        Then comes Shelley
Bearing a letter from his wife, denying
That Claire and Shelley loved, you understand —
By the flesh.   Sweet, was it not?   Naïve!
This letter I should hand the Hoppners, who
Believed the story, and who held a place
Persuasive touching poor Allegra.   Well,
So Shelley comes and makes the point, the child
Is in ill health, Claire, too, in a decline,
And hands this letter to me for the Hoppners.

LORD BYRON TO DOCTOR POLIDORI

And I've misplaced it.   Frankly, from the first,
Had no fixed purpose to deliver it.
What principle makes me collaborator
With such fantastic business?   To resume:
He acted like the boy he was.   I smiled —
Against the flaming rage that burned his face —
My mocking smile, he thought, the Don Juan
Upcurved my lips.   I read his very thought
Between words spoken; words that he suppressed:
It was that I was glad that Claire was ill
Because of that male mood when love of man
Finds sustenance where suffering lays low
The object of desire: If she suffers,
The man subdues, devours her.   She escapes
If free of love.   Oh yes, and this he thought:
That I was glad she suffered, since my glory
Had failed to hold her, failed to satisfy
Her noble heart!   God's wounds!   Why Shelley thought
She turned to him and with his spirit found
A purity of peace and sweetest friendship,
And faith that saves and serves, as men and women
Are to each other souls to serve and save!
Poor fool!   I read it all, or pieced it out
With words that I picked up from time to time. . . .

There was this further thing: I am a man,
So say they, who accepts the dying creed
That woman's love is lawless and a toy
When given if no priest has sanctified it —
Not quite, perhaps.   The point is further on.

STARVED ROCK

In any case 'tis this: that this belief,
Mine or part mine, and coloring my acts,
Shadowed no whit the brow of Lady Claire.
And that I, greatest lover of my time,
Had won this lady's body but to lose
The lady's soul, a soul that slipped and fled
Out of the hands that clasped her flesh, because
She knew me through her gift, thought less of me,
And no wise felt herself bound to my life
Because she gave her body. Kept her mind,
Soul, free, untouched by that gift, by the gift
Was cognizant of what is false and poor —
(I use some words I heard) in me. And thus
I lost her soul, though earlier I had gained
What seemed all to me, all I had the genius
To comprehend in woman! Then comes Shelley
And finds her soul, the genuine prize, and I
Grow sullen with a consciousness of vision
Inferior to his. All this they thought.
Oh Jesus, what a lie!

I have loved Nature, love her now: and woman
Is Nature, and my love for nature means
Inclusion of the sex. I have not soared
To heights that sickened me and made me laugh
At what I sought — or turned from it. No moons
Behind the clouds; no terrors and no symbols,
No Emilia Vivianni's have I had.
I know, believe me, love for woman calls

LORD BYRON TO DOCTOR POLIDORI

A man's soul up to heights too rare to live in.
I have not risen, therefore, will not rise
Where thinking stops, because the blood leaves brain
Therefore have had no falls, and no recoils
Chasing the Plato vision, the star, the wonder,
The beauty and the terror, harmony
Of nature's art; the passion that would make
The loved one of the self-same womb with me,
A sister, spouse or angel, dæmon, pilot
Of life and fate.

> How much of truth is here?

Dreams seen most vividly by Petrarch, Dante,
Who loved without achievement, balking nature,
Till Passion, like an involute, pressed in
Harder and harder on its starving leaves,
Becomes a fragrance — sublimate of self
Sucked out of sorrow's earth, at last becomes
A meditative madness.   All is written
Fairly across my page.   " She walks in beauty: "
" When we two parted," " Could love like a river,"
" Bright be the place of thy soul."   Lines, lines
In " Harold," " Don Juan."   Yes, I have loved,
But saw how far love lures, how far to venture,
Knowing what can and what cannot be made
Of the mystery, the wonder, therefore never
Have had to laugh at self; find Vivianni
A housemaid shelling corn — not threading pearls.

Or sit, with idiot eyes, my bones half broken,
Icarus bumped amid a field of stones.

I know the hour of farewell.   I have said it
When my heart trembled, stopped as when a horse
Braces its terrored feet to keep from plunging
Over the precipice.   Farewell!   Farewell!
I know to say, and turn, and pass my way.

Why!   For that matter, even now behold!
Do I feel less than Shelley would in this?
I leave the Countess for the war in Greece.
What's done is done.   What's lived is lived.   Come,
    Doctor,
Let's practice with the pistols.   Mother of God,
What is this thing called Life?

THE FOLDING MIRROR

A folding mirror! What may it be?
Nothing? Or something? Let me see!
Its silver chain is hung to the sky
On a planet nail. And it fronts my eye.
No stars reflect themselves at first,
The mirrors are dustless, vacant and clean.
Not even my face shows — am I cursed?
What may the mirrors mean?

     *   *   *   *   *

I watch like a cat that waits to mangle
A breathless rat in an alley nook.
And a little figure steps into the angle
Made by the folding mirrors.   Look!
His thin legs wobble, bend and dangle
Like radish roots.   He takes the crook
Out of his arms and raises them up,
As if in panic, or supplication.
He bends and peers, whines like a pup,
Walks to and fro in his desperation,
Pinches his arms and beats his breast;
Runs quivering fingers between his hair,
Wavers for weariness, sighs for rest,
Looks up to the planet that seems to bear
The silver chain like a brad in the wall.

STARVED ROCK

Upsprings, searches the mirrors again;
Sees for the first the prodigal
Waste of stars in the black inane.
Stamps with his feet upon the void
He stands on, paces on, why, he wonders
Is he upborned like an asteroid?
Hark! The limitless blackness thunders:
The Infinite growls, he whirls and shivers,
Runs to cover the mirrors to climb.
They yield like the waters of phantom rivers.
He acts like a soul new born that quivers
Before the mirrors of Space and Time.

*　　*　　*　　*　　*

Now what's to do? He must fill in.
This emptiness with horror is shod.
When did this pageant of things begin?
Somewhere hiding there is a God.
Some one drove that planet nail
Into the blue wall; some one hung
The silver chain. And what is the tale
Of the mirrors here in the blackness swung?
The soul is naked, weak and alone,
And sees its nakedness in the glass.
It must create from wood and stone,
Wire and reeds, color and brass.
It must create though it be but a mime,
Make a reality all its own
Before the mirror of white called Time,
Before the mirror of blue called Space.

THE FOLDING MIRROR

Clasp the vastness between their folds,
Find laws, raise altars, dream of a face —
Make that real which the hope beholds.

     *   *   *   *   *

Our terrored manikin commences,
Fattens his littleness with clothes.
With crowns and miters puffs his senses,
Crushes the grape to drown his woes.
Fills full the mirrors with faces. Now
They are dancing before them, age and youth,
Laurels or thorns are bound on a brow.
They hunt and slay for a thing called Truth.
Dig for treasure, toil for riches,
Struggle for place — it is well enough!
Some lift their busts into chosen niches.
All are hungry for peace and love.
And only a few are blind, dispute
The thing is a dream. If there be worth
It lies in the strings of the lyre or lute,
Sounds that never return to earth;
Dreams to seeing eyes reflected,
Caught from infinite realms afar.
How could they be seen, or recollected
Except for the Real — except for a Star?

     *   *   *   *   *

God in the blackness, whirlwind, lightning,
God in the blinding fire of the sun
Before these empty mirrors brightening
See what we do, what we have done!

STARVED ROCK

Out of an astral substance molding
Music and laws for our hearts' control,
Yes, and a hope that the mirrors' folding
Lets slip through a growing soul.
Are you not proud of us, do you not pity?
Is all the glory thine alone?
Then if it be, you must take the city
Builded, demolished stone from stone.
All of our madness, weariness, error,
Blindness, weakness, pain and loss,
Fumbling feebly before the mirror,
Yours is the crown, but yours the cross!
Yours is the juice of grape or poppies
To fill the void with a make believe;
Yours the hope where never a prop is,
The opiates, too, that dull, deceive,
No less than nature that lifts eternal
Vision of Life to quiet the heart:
Verse and color that stamp the infernal
Dragon of Fear with the feet of Art.
Yours and ours the consolations
In loneliness and in terror wrought
Out of our spirits' desolations,
Out of our spirits' love and thought!

A WOMAN OF FORTY

Eyes that have long looked on the world,
Taken and stored the soul of outward things,
Dread to look on themselves,
In the mirror to gaze upon their mirrorings!

There to behold what time has done, what thought
Has changed their look and light.
I have lost my face through sorrow and dreams
And dare not find it, lest it smite

This self to-day, since I may not restore
My old self who in gladness without terror
Beheld and knew myself
Each morning in the mirror!

In the long quest of love I may have found
A spirit after whom my passion lusted.
But I had trust not giving love,
I have given love to hearts I have not trusted.

One thing has come that I would never see,
Hidden or trembling in my eyes:
Love in the mirror shown fatigued and mild,
Hopeless and wise.

[33]

WILD BIRDS

The wild birds among the reeds
Cry, exult and stretch their wings.
Out of the sky they drift
And sink to the water's rushes.
But the wild birds beat their wings and cry
To the newcomer out of the sky!

Is he a stranger, this wild bird out of the sky?
Or do they cry to him because of remembered places
And remembered days
Spent together
In the north-land, or the south-land?

Is this the ecstasy of renewal,
Or the ecstasy of beginning?
For the wild bird touches his bill
Against a mate;
He brushes her wing with his wing;
He quivers with delight
For the cool sky of blue,
And the touch of her wing!

The wild birds fly up from the reeds of the water,
Some for the south,

WILD BIRDS

Some for the north.
They are gone —
Lost in the sky!

In what water do these mates of a morning
Exult on the morrow?
What wild birds will cry to them as they sink
Out of an unknown sky?
To whose cry will she quiver
Through her burnished wings to-morrow,
In the north-land,
In the south-land,
Far away?

A LADY

She sleeps beneath a canopy of carnation silk,
Embroidered with Venetian lace,
Between linens that crush in the hand
Soft as down.
Waking, she looks through a window
Curtained with carnation silk,
Embroidered with Venetian lace,
The walls are hung with velvet
Embossed with a *fleur de lis,*
And around her is the silence of richness,
Where foot-falls are like exhalations
From carpets of moss.
Little clocks tinkle.
Medallions priceless as jewels
Lie by jars suspiring like coals of fire.
And a maid prepares the bath,
Tincturing delicious water with exquisite essences.
And she is served with coffee
In cups as thin as petals,
Sitting amid pillows that breathe
The souls of freesia!

All things are hers:
Fishes from all seas,

A LADY

Fruits from all climes.
The city lies at her command,
And is summoned by buttons
Which are pressed for her.
Noiselessly feet move on many floors,
Serving her.
Wheels that turn under coaches
Of crystal and ebony,
And yachts dreaming in strange waters,
And wings — all are hers!
And she is free:
Her husband comes and goes
From his suite below hers.
She never sees him,
Nor knows his ways, nor his days.

But she is very weary
And all alone amid her servants,
And guests that come and go.
Her lips are red,
Her skin is soft and smooth —
But the page blurs before her eyes.
Her eyelids are languid,
And droop from weariness,
Though she will not rest
From the long pursuit of love!
Her hair is white;
The skin of her faultless neck
Edges in creases

STARVED ROCK

As she turns her perfect head.
And the days dawn and die.
What day that dawns will bring her love?
And day by day she waits for the dawn
Of a new life, a great love!

But every morning brings its remembrance
Of the increasing years that are gone.
And every evening brings its fear
Of death which must come,
Until her nerves are shaken
Like a woman's hair in the wind —
What must be done?
Some one tells her that God is love.
And when the fears come
She says to self over and over,
" God is love!   God is love!
All is well."
And she wins a little oblivion,
Through saying " God is love,"
From the truth in her heart which cries:
" Love is life,
Love is a lover,
And love is God! "

She is a flower
Which the spring has nourished,
And the summer exhausted.
Fall is at hand.
Weird zephyrs stir her leaves and blossoms;

A LADY

And she says to herself, " It is not fall,
For God is love! "

My poor flower!
May this therapy ease you into sleep,
And the folding of jewelless hands!
You are beginning to be sick
Of the incurable disease of age,
And the weariness of futile flesh!

THE NEGRO WARD

Scarce had I written: it were best
To crush this love, to give you up,
Drink at one draught the bitter cup,
And kill this new life in my breast,
Than Parker's breathing seemed to give
Ominous sound the end was near.
I did so want this man to live —
This negro soldier, dear.

'Twas three in the morning, all was still
But Parker's rattle in the throat,
Outside I heard the whippoorwill.
The new moon like an Indian boat
Hung just above the darkened grove,
Where you and I had pledged our love,
When you were here.   Such precious hours,
Such fleeting moments then were ours . . .
Alone here in the silent ward,
With Parker dying, I was scared.
His breath came short, his lips were blue.
I asked him: " Is there something more,
Parker, that I can do for you?"
" Please hold my hand," he said.   Before
I took it, it was growing cold —
Death, how quick it comes!

THE NEGRO WARD

Then next I seemed to hear the drums —
For I had fainted for his eyes
That stared with such a wide surprise,
As the lids fell apart they stared,
As if they saw what to behold
Had startled his poor soul which fared
Where it would not.   I heard the drums,
The bugle next, lay there so faint
With Parker's eyes still in my view,
Like bubble motes which flit and paint
Themselves upon the heaven's blue.
An orderly had mailed meanwhile
That letter, to you, there I lay
Too weak to write again, unsay
What I had written.

                              Down the aisle,
Between our beds a step I heard,
A voice: "Our order's here, we leave
In half an hour for France."   I stirred
Like a dead thing, could scarce conceive
What tragedy was come.   No chance
To write you or to telegraph.
In twelve hours more, as in a trance
I looked from Ellis Island, where
My chums could gayly talk and laugh.
In two hours more we sailed for France.
All this was hard, but still to bear
The knowledge of you, your despair,

Or change, or bitterness, if you thought
That letter came from me, was wrought
Out of a heart that could not stake
Its own blood for your sake.

I will come back to you at length
If I but live and have the strength.
How will you like me with hair white,
And wasted cheeks, deep lined and pale?
It all began that dreadful night
Of Parker's death, the strain and fright,
The letter it seemed best to write —
From then to now I have been frail.
Our ship just missed a submarine,
And here the hardships, gas-gangrene,
The horrors and the deaths have stripped
My life of everything. Is it to prove
For duty, you, though bloody-lipped,
And fallen my unconquerable love
For country and for you through all,
Whatever fate befall?

What is my soul's great anguish for?
For what this tragedy of war?
For what the fate that says to us:
Part hands and be magnanimous?
For what the judgment which decrees
The mother love in me to cease?
For separation, hopeless miles
Of land and water us between?

THE NEGRO WARD

For what the devil force that smiles
At man's immedicable pain?

I have not lost my faith in God.
Life has grown dark, I only say:
Dear God, my feet have lost the way.
Religion, wisdom do not give
A place to stand, a space to live.
I have not lost my faith in love,
That somehow it must rise above
The clouds of earth, I still can rest
In dreams sometimes upon your breast.
But, oh, it seems sometimes a play
Where gods are picking a bouquet:
The blossom of war, my soul or yours
More fragrant grown as it endures. . . .

WILLIAM SHAKSPEARE

Homer saw nations, armies, multitudes —
You saw them in the intimate interludes
Of Brutus' soul at midnight in a tent
When the infection festers the event.
Ulysses' course is changed by the sea's trough.
You saw an epoch when a hat blows off.
Orestes fled the Furies, won his peace
Through Apollo in old Greece.
But who unbars the mouse traps of your world,
Or kills the ambushed serpent where it's curled?
Your Fates return, and Fortinbras draws in
On Hamlet's impotence and Gertrude's sin.
All oceans in a raindrop, drops of dew
Containing perfect heavens starred and blue;
Angels who mother Calibans, and hopes
Are of your vision — great mosaics hued
With thoughts of princes, poets, misanthropes,
Reveal their minute colors closer viewed.
Atomies, maggots, worms or gilded flies,
Nothing too small or foul is for your eyes.
You made a culture of dreams lost or won
Like Robert Browning, Emily Dickinson.
You looked in heaven when the lightning shone,
Then saw a fairy's whip of cricket bone.
For gods and men bacteriologist

WILLIAM SHAKSPEARE

Of spiritual microbes hidden which subsist
In moments of red joy — calm satirist
Of worlds forsaken for a woman's hair,
Kings slain, states crumbled, heroes false or fair,
The madness of the flesh, love on the wrack,
A white maid married to a soldier black.
Incests, adulteries and secret sins,
The fall of monarchs and of manikins.
All men at last a rattling empty pod,
All men destroyed like flies for sport of God.
All Life at last an idiot's furious tale —
You had the strength to say this and not quail!
For you what were the unities, the rules
Of Plautus, Corneille or the Grecian schools?
Flame through a pipe will sing, perhaps, when blown
Against the craftsman's silver, but the tone
Of worlds in conflagration, that's to be
The sacred fire with wings outspread and free,
Wherein an Athens falls, a Sidon stands,
And where a freezing clown may warm his hands.

If you could empty out a tiger's brain
And wire up its spinal cord again
To Sappho's brain, it would no doubt devour
The tiger's nerves and sinews in an hour.
Such muscles and such bones could not endure
The avid hunger of a fire so pure.
And you, Will Shakspeare, spirit sensitive,
You lived past fifty, that is long to live
And feed a flame like yours, and let the flame

STARVED ROCK

Remake itself and lap at flesh and frame.
I say with Jesus, wisdom's eyes are blind
To seek a poet out and think to find
A slender reed that's shaken by the wind.
Come cyclops of the counter, millionaires,
Lawyers and statesmen in the world's affairs,
And thin away like flesh which acid eats
Under the passion even of John Keats.
But if you felt and saw love, agony,
As Shakspeare knew them you would quickly die.
There is no tragedy like the gift of song,
It keeps you mortal but demands you strong;
It gives you God's eyes blurred with human tears,
And crowns a thousand lives in fifty years.
Enter the breathless silence where God dwells,
See and record all heavens and all hells!

FOR A PLAY

Love began with both of them so gently
Meeting, neither thought nor looked intently.
Afterward her breath invoked the fire —
Breath to breath set burning their desire.

Is there aught in flesh or is it spirit
Conscious of its kindred soul when near it?
Woe to flesh or soul that's wholly wakened
While the other's soul-depths lie unshakened!

How could she give him all sacred blisses,
Long embraces, in the darkness kisses,
If she was not his, all else forgetting,
Lovers gone and other loves' regretting?

That was just the place her gold was leadened —
Flesh there too alive, to him all deadened.
She could harp not to his playing wholly,
Yet his heart strings trembled for her solely.

So this love play hastened to the curtain.
Each one spoke his lines in accents certain,
While at times behind the wings her glances
Warmed the prompter's treasonous advances.

STARVED ROCK

Is there greater martydom than this is?
You have staked your soul where the abyss is.
You have given all — oh sorry barter
You have lit the fire for you the martyr.

You will still love on, or turn to hating,
Days depart, your heart stays in its waiting,
Where's the blame?   She gave her heart's half measure,
All she had, for all your soul's full treasure.

What's the half to keep, could you achieve it?
What your treasure if you could retrieve it?
Never more shall you again bestow it . . .
Now you have a song if you're a poet.

Now you're ever dumb if song's denied you,
You shall be more dumb than all beside you,
While your soul is shaken by its torrents —
Dante songless in a Dante Florence.

Age shall not make strong, nor deeper learning.
Grief grows clearer with your eye's discerning.
Pass the years, but oh the soil grows faster —
Richer for the roots of your disaster.

Ends the play — for what is life but dying?
What is love but fire forever crying?
What your soul but love's pure carbon fuel?
Love and life make ashes of the jewel!

CHICAGO

On the gray paper of this mist and fog
With dust for the erasure and with smoke
For drawing crayons, be this charcoal scrawl:
The breed of Gog in the kingdom of Magog,
Skyscrapers, helmeted, stand sentinel
Amid the obscuring fumes of coal and coke,
Raised by enchantment out of the sand and bog.
This sky-line, the Sierras of the lake,
Cuts with dulled teeth,
Which twist and break,
The imponderable and drifting steam.
And restlessly beneath
This man-created mountain chain,
Like the flow of a prairie river
Endlessly by day and night, forever
Along the boulevards pedestrians stream
In a shuffle like dancers to a low refrain:
Forever by day and night
Pursuing as of old the lure of delight,
And the ghosts of pleasure or pain.
Their rhythmic feet sound like the falling of rain,
Or the hush of the waves, when the roar
Is blown by a wind off shore.

STARVED ROCK

II

From a tower like a mountain promontory
The cesspool of a railroad lies to view
Fouling the marble of the city's glory:
A crapulous sluice of garbage and of cars
Where engines rush and whistle, smudge the blue
With filth like the trail of slugs.
It is a trench of steel which bars
Free access to the common shore, and hugs
In a coil of lazar arms the boulevard.
Cattle and hogs delivered here for slaughter
Corrupt the loveliness of the water front.
They low and grunt,
Switched back and forth within the tangled yard.
But from this tower the amethystine water,
The water of jade or slate,
Is visible with its importunate
Gestures against the sky to still retreats
In Michigan, of quiet woods and hills
Beyond the simmering passion of these streets,
And all their endless ills. . . .

III

But over the switch yard stands the Institute
Guarded by lions on the avenue,
Colossal lions standing for attack;
Between whose feet luminous and resolute
Children of the city passing through

CHICAGO

To palettes, compasses, the demoniac
Spirit of the city shall subdue.
Lions are in the loop and jackals too.
They have no trainers but the alderman,
Who uses them to hunt with, but in time
The city shall behold its nobler plan
Achieved by hands that rhyme,
Workers who architect and build,
And out of thought its substance re-arrange,
Till all its prophecies shall be fulfilled.
Through numbers, science and art
The city shall know change,
And win dominion over water and light,
The cyclop's mastery of the mart;
The devils overcome,
Which stalk the squalid ways by night
Of poverty and the slum,
Where the crook is spawned, the burglar and the bum.
These youths who pass the lions shall assuage
The city's thirst and hunger,
And save it from the wastage and the wage
Of the demagogue, the precinct monger.

IV

This is the city of great doges hidden
In guarded offices and country places.
The city strives against the things forbidden
By the doges, on whose faces
The city at large never looks;

STARVED ROCK

Doges who could accomplish if they would
In a month the city's beauty and good.
Yet this city in a hundred years has risen
Out of a haunt of foxes, wolves and rooks,
And breaks asunder now the bars of the prison
Of dead days and dying.   It has spread
For many a rood its boundaries, like the sprawled
And fallen Hephaestos, and has tenanted
Its neighborhoods increasing and unwalled
With peoples from all lands.
From Milwaukee Avenue to the populous mills
Of South Chicago, from the Sheridan Drive
Through forests where the water smiles
To Harlem for miles and miles.
It reaches out its hands,
Powerful and alive
With dreams to touch tomorrow, which it wills
To dawn and which shall dawn. . . .
And like lights that twinkle through the stench
And putrid mist of abattoirs,
Great souls are here, separate and withdrawn,
Companionless, whom darkness cannot quench.
Seeing they are the chrysalis which must feed
Upon its own thoughts and the life to be,
Its flight among the stars.
Beauty is here, like half protected flowers,
Blooms and will cast its multiplying seed,
Until one mass of color shall succeed
The shaley places of these arid hours.

CHICAGO

V

Chicago! by this inland sea
In the land of Lincoln, in the state
Of souls who held the nation's fate,
City both old and young, I consecrate
Your future years to truth and liberty.
Be this the record frail and incomplete
Of one who saw you, mingled with the masses
Along these magical mountain passes
With restless yet with hopeful feet.
Could they return to see you who have slept
These fifty years, who laid your first foundations!
And oh! could we behold you who have kept
Their promises for you, when new generations
Shall walk this boulevard made fair
In chiseled marble, looking at the lake
Of clearer water under a bluer air.
We who shall sleep then nor awake,
Have left the labor to you and the care
Ask great fulfillment, for ourselves a prayer!

THE WEDDING FEAST

Said the chief of the marriage feast to the groom,
  Whence is this blood of the vine?
Men serve at first the best, he said,
  And at the last, poor wine.

Said the chief of the marriage feast to the groom,
  When the guests have drunk their fill
They drink whatever wine you serve,
  Nor know the good from the ill.

How have you kept the good till now
  When our hearts nor care nor see?
Said the chief of the marriage feast to the groom,
  Whence may this good wine be?

Said the chief of the marriage feast, this wine
  Is the best of all by far.
Said the groom, there stand six jars without
  And the wine fills up each jar.

Said the chief of the marriage feast, we lacked
  Wine for the wedding feast.
How comes it now one jar of wine
  To six jars is increased?

[54]

THE WEDDING FEAST

Who makes our cup to overflow?
    And who has the wedding blest?
Said the groom to the chief of the feast, a stranger
    Is here as a wedding guest.

Said the groom to the chief of the wedding feast,
    Moses by power divine
Smote water at Meribah from the rock,
    But this man makes us wine.

Said the groom to the chief of the wedding feast,
    Elisha by power divine
Made oil for the widow to sell for bread,
    But this man, wedding wine.

He changed the use of the jars, he said,
    From an outward rite and sign:
Where water stood for the washing of feet,
    For heart's delight there's wine.

So then 'tis he, said the chief of the feast,
    Who the wedding feast has blest?
Said the groom to the chief of the feast, the stranger
    Is the merriest wedding guest.

He laughs and jests with the wedding guests,
    He drinks with the happy bride.
Said the chief of the wedding feast to the groom,
    Go bring him to my side.

STARVED ROCK

Jesus of Nazareth came up,
    And his body was fair and slim.
Jesus of Nazareth came up,
    And his mother came with him.

Jesus of Nazareth stands with the dancers
    And his mother by him stands.
The bride kneels down to Jesus of Nazareth
    And kisses his rosy hands.

The bridegroom kneels to Jesus of Nazareth
    And Jesus blesses the twain.
I go a way, said Jesus of Nazareth,
    Of darkness, sorrow and pain.

After the wedding feast is labor,
    Suffering, sickness, death,
And so I make you wine for the wedding,
    Said Jesus of Nazareth.

My heart is with you, said Jesus of Nazareth,
    As the grape is one with the vine.
Your bliss is mine, said Jesus of Nazareth,
    And so I make you wine.

Youth and love I bless, said Jesus,
    Song and the cup that cheers.
The rosy hands of Jesus of Nazareth
    Are wet with the young bride's tears.

THE WEDDING FEAST

Love one another, said Jesus of Nazareth,
    Ere cometh the evil of years.
The rosy hands of Jesus of Nazareth
    Are wet with the bridegroom's tears.

Jesus of Nazareth goes with his mother,
    The dancers are dancing again.
There's a woman who pauses without to listen,
    'Tis Mary Magdalen.

Forth to the street a Scribe from the wedding
    Goes with a Sadducee.
Said the Scribe, this shows how loose a fellow
    Can come out of Galilee!

BY THE WATERS OF BABYLON

By the waters of Babylon by the sea,
On the sand where the waters died,
The sea wind and the tide
Drowned the words you spoke to me.

The sea fell at our feet.   The sand
Hushed the whispering waters, near
The babble of boats by the pier
Was the ictus to the roar on the strand.

By the waters of Babylon a grief to be,
The waiting ships in the bay,
Awed the words we would say
Against the sound of the sea:

For France was below the waters, and the west
Behind me where the rains
Come in November on the window panes,
And the blast shakes the ruined nest

Under the dripping eaves.   What then remains
But memory of the waters of Babylon,
And the ships like swan after swan,
Under the drone of angry hydroplanes?

BY THE WATERS OF BABYLON

By the waters of Babylon we did not weep,
Though love comes and is gone,
As the wind is, as waters drawn
In spray from the deep.

Neither for things foreseen and ominous,
For newer hands that somewhere wait
To thrill afresh, the reblossomed fate
Did we surrender dolorous. . . .

Change now is yours beyond the waters, nights
Of waiting and of doubt have dimmed desire.
Our hands are calm before the dying fire
Of lost delights.

Babylon by the sea knows us no more.
Between the surge's hushes
When on the sand the water rushes
There is no voice of ours upon the shore.

THE DREAM OF TASSO

O Earth that walls these prison bars — O Stones
Which shut my body in — could I be free
If these fell and the grated door which groans
For every back scourged hither oped for me?
Freedom were what to travel you, O Earth,
When my heart makes its daily agony?
And longing such as mine cannot ungirth
Its bands and its mortality o'erleap.
Our life is love unsatisfied from birth,
Our life is longing waking or asleep,
And mine has been a vigil of quick pain.
O Leonora, thus it is I keep
Grief in my heart and weariness of brain.

How did I know these chains and bars are wrought
Of frailer stuff than space, that I could gain
In earth no respite, but a vision brought
The truth, O Leonora? It was this:
I dreamed this hopeless love, so long distraught
Was never caged, but from the first was bliss,
And moved like music from the meeting hour
To the rapt moment of the earliest kiss
Bestowed upon your hands, to gathering flower
Of lips so purely yielded, the embrace
Tender as dawn in April when a shower

THE DREAM OF TASSO

Quenches with gentleness each flowering place;
So were your tears of gladness — so my hands
Which stroked your golden hair, your sunny face,
Even as flying clouds o'er mountain lands
Caress with fleeting love the morning sun.

Now I was with you, and by your commands.
Your love was mine at last completely won,
And waited but the blossom. How you sang,
Laughed, ran about your palace rooms and none
Closed doors against me, desks and closets sprang
To my touch open, all your secrets lay
Revealed to me in gladness — and this pang
Which I had borne in bitterness day by day
Was gone, nor could I bring it back, or think
How it had been, or why — this heart so gay
In sudden sunshine could no longer link
Itself with what it was.

                    Look! Every room
Had blooms your hands had gathered white and pink,
And drained from precious vases their perfume.
And fruits were heaped for me in golden bowls,
And tapestries from many an Asian loom
Were hung for me, and our united souls
Shone over treasure books — how glad you were
To listen to my epic, from the scrolls
Of Jerusalem, the holy sepulcher.
Still as a shaft of light you sat and heard
With veilèd eyes which tears could scarcely blur,

But flowed upon your cheek with every word.
And your hand reached for mine — you did not speak,
But let your silence tell how you were stirred
By love for me and wonder! What to seek
In earth and heaven more? Heaven at last
Was mine on earth, and for a sacred week
This heaven all of heaven.

                                    So it passed
This week with you — you served me ancient wine.
We sat across a table where you cast
A cloth of chikku, or we went to dine
There in the stately room of heavy plate.
Or tiring of the rooms, the day's decline
Beheld us by the river to await
The evening planet, where in elfin mood
You whistled like the robin to its mate,
And won its answering call. Then through the wood
We wandered back in silence hand in hand,
And reached the sacred portal with our blood
Running so swift no ripples stirred the sand
To figures of reflection.

                                    Once again
Within your room of books, upon the stand
The reading lights are brought to us, and then
You read to me from Plato, and my heart
Breathes like a bird at rest; the world of men,
Strife, hate, are all forgotten in this art
Of life made perfect. Or when weariness

THE DREAM OF TASSO

Comes over us, you dim the lamp and start
The blue light back of Dante's bust to bless
Our twilight with its beauty.

                        So the time
Passes too quickly — our poor souls possess
Beauty and love a moment — and our rhyme
Which captures it, creates the illusion love
Has permanence, when even at its prime
Decay has taken it from the light above,
Or darkness underneath.

                       I must recur
To our first sleep and all the bliss thereof.
How did you first come to me, how confer
On me your beauty? That first night it was
The blue light back of Dante, but a blur
Of golden light our spirits, when you pass
Your hand across my brow, our souls go out
To meet each other, leave as wilted grass
Our emptied bodies. Then we grow devout,
And kneel and pray together for the gift
Of love from heaven, and to banish doubt
Of change or faithlessness. Then with a swift
Arising from the prayer you disappear.
I sleep meanwhile, you come again and lift
My head against your bosom, bringing near
A purple robe for me, and say, "Wear this,
And to your chamber go." And thus I hear,
And leave you; on my couch, where calm for bliss

STARVED ROCK

I wait for you and listen, hear your feet
Whisper their secret to the tapestries
Of your ecstatic coming — O my sweet!
I touched your silken gown, where underneath
Your glowing flesh was dreaming, made complete
My rapture by upgathering, quick of breath,
Your golden ringlets loosened — and at last
Hold you in love's embrace — would it were Death! . . .
For soon 'twixt love and sleep the night was past,
And dawn cob-webbed the chamber.   Then I heard
One faintest note and all was still — the vast
Spherule of heaven was pecked at by a bird
As it were to break the sky's shell, let the light
Of morning flood the fragments scattered, stirred
By breezes of the dawn with passing night.
We woke together, heard together, thrilled
With speechless rapture!   Were your spirit's plight
As mine is with this vision, had I willed
To torture you with absence?   Would I save
Your spirit if its anguish could be stilled
Only among the worms that haunt the grave?

My dream goes on a little: Day by day,
These seven days we lived together, gave
Our spirits to each other.   With dismay
You watched my hour's departure.   On you crept
Light shadows after moments sunny, gay.
But when the hour was come, you sat and wept,
And said to me: " I hear the rattling clods
Upon the coffin of our love."   You stepped

THE DREAM OF TASSO

And stood beside the casement, said " A god's
Sarcophagus this room will be as soon
As you have gone, and mine shall be the rod's
Bitterness of memory both night and noon
Amid the silence of this palace."   So
I spoke and said, " If you would have the boon —
O Leonora, do I live to know
This hope too passionate made consummate? —
Yet if it be I shall return, nor go
But to return to you, and make our fate
Bound fast for life."   How happy was your smile,
Your laughter soon,— and then from door to gate
I passed and left you, to be gone awhile
Around Ferrara.

                                      In three days, it seemed,
I came again, and as I walked each mile
Counting to self — my feet lagged as I dreamed —
And said ten miles, nine miles, eight miles, at last
One mile, so many furlongs, then I dreamed
Your reading lamps were lighted for me, cast
Their yellow beams upon the mid-night air.
But oh my heart which stopped and stood aghast
To see the lamp go out and note the glare
Of blue light set behind the Dante mask!
Who wore my robe of purple false and fair?
Who drank your precious vintage from the flask
Roman and golden whence I drank so late?
Who held you in his arms and thus could ask?
Receive your love?   Mother of God!   What fate

STARVED ROCK

Was mine beneath the darkness of that sky,
There at your door who could not leave or wait,
And heard the bird of midnight's desolate cry?
And saw at last the blue light quenched, and saw
A taper lighted in my chamber — why
This treachery, Leonora? Why withdraw
The love you gave, or eviler, lead me here,
O sorceress, before whom heaven's law
Breaks and is impotent — whose eyes no tear
Of penitence shall know, whose spirit fares
Free, without consequence, as a child could sear
Its fellow's hands with flame, or unawares,
Or with premeditation, and then laugh and turn
Upon its play. For you, light heart, no snares
Or traps of conscience wait, who thus could spurn
A love invited.

                    Thus about your lawn
I listened till the stars had ceased to burn,
But when I saw the imminence of the dawn
And heard our bird cry, I could stand no more,
My heart broke and I fled and wandered on
Down through the valley by the river's shore.
For when the bird cried, did you wake with him?
Did you two gaze as we had gazed before
Upon that blissful morning? I was dim
Of thought and spirit, by the river lay
Watching the swallows over the water skim,
And plucking leaves from weeds to turn or stay
The madness of my life's futility,

THE DREAM OF TASSO

Grown blank as that terrific dawn — till day
Flooded upon me, noon came, what should be?
Where should I go? What prison chains could rest
So heavily on the spirit, as that free,
But vast and ruined world?

                 O arrowed breast
Of me, your Tasso! And you came and drew
The arrows out which kept the blood repressed,
And let my wounds the freer bleed: 'Twas you
By afternoon who walked upon an arm
More lordly than mine is. You stopped nor knew,
I saw him take your body lithe and warm
Close to his breast, yes, even where we had stood
Upon our day, embraced — feed on the charm
Of widened eyes and swiftly coursing blood.
I watched you walk away and disappear
In the deep verdure of the river wood,
Too faint to rise and fly, crushed by the fear
Of madness, sudden death!

               This was my dream,
From which I woke and saw again the sheer
Walls of my prison, which no longer seem
The agony they did, even though the cell
Is the hard penalty and the cursed extreme
Hate in return for love. But oh you hell,
You boundless earth to wander in and brood —
Great prison house of grief in which to dwell,
Remembering love forgotten, pride subdued,

STARVED ROCK

And love desired and found and lost again.
That is the prison which no fortitude
Can suffer, and the never dying pain
From which the spacious luring of the earth
Tempts flight for spirit freedom, but in vain!

Ah Leonora! Even from our birth
We build our prisons! What are walls like these
Beside the walls of memory, or the dearth
Of hope in all this life, the agonies
Of spiritual chains and gloom? I suffer less,
Imprisoned thus, than if the memories
Of love bestowed and love betrayed should press
Round my unresting steps. And I send up
To heaven thanks that spared that bitterness,
That garden of the soul's reluctant cup!

THE CHRISTIAN STATESMAN

He hears his father pray when he's a boy:
" Jesus we know, the Savior, and we ask,
In Thy great plenitude of mercy, grace,
Forgiveness for our waywardness; we invoke
Thy blessing, and may righteousness and peace
Prevail in all the earth. Meekly we rest
Upon the precious promise of Thy word.
Gather us home with Thine own people, Lord,
And all the glory shall be Thine."

                                        So much
To show the father's prayer which he heard.
The father is a saint, a quietist,
Save that he has his hatreds, strong enough:
Turns face of stone and silence to the men
Whose ways of life are laid in sin, he thinks
And calls them dirty dogs and scalawags,
Because they vote a ticket he dislikes,
Or love a game of cards, a glass of beer,
Or go to see the County Fair, where once
A drunken bus-man drives upon a boy
And kills him. Then the saint is all aflame,
And tries to have the fair put out for good.

And so the son, who will become at last
The Christian Statesman, hears his father pray,
And prays himself, and takes the lesson in
Of godliness, the Bible as the source
Of truth infallible, divine.

                          This boy
Is blessed with health, a body without flaw,
His forehead is a little low, perhaps,
And has a transverse dent which keeps the brain
Shaped to the skull; a perfect brain is sphered,
As perfect things are circles; but a brain
Something below perfection, which is fed
By a great body and an obdurate will,
And sense of moral purpose will go far,
Farther than better brains in craft of states,
For some years anyway, if a voice be given
Which reaches to the largest crowded room,
To speak the passionate moralities
Which come into that brain creased straight across
The forehead with a dent.

                        He goes to school,
And from the first believes he has a mission
To make the world a better place, avows
His mission in the world, bends all his strength
To make his armor ready: health of body,
A blameless life, hard studies, practices
With word and voice.

[70]

THE CHRISTIAN STATESMAN

It is a country college
Where he matriculates — the father wished it;
A college where the boys are mostly poor,
And waste no time, have not the cash to buy
Delight, if they desired.

He ruminates
Upon the pebbles and Demosthenes,
And sets his will to be an orator
That he may herald truth and save the world.
After much toil, re-writing, he delivers
A speech he calls, " Ich Dien," and loses out
Against a youth who speaks on Liberty.
And then he uses Gladstone for his theme,
The Christian Statesman; for exordium
Tells of the ermine which will die before
It suffers soilure — that was Gladstone — yes!
But still he cannot win the prize; a boy
Who talks about the labors of Charles Darwin,
His suffering and sacrifice, is awarded
The prize this time — a boy who had the wit
To speak in praise of Darwin's virtues — saying
Nothing about his hellish doctrines, thus
Winning the cautious judges to his theme.

But is our little Gladstone crushed, dismayed?
He plucks up further strength and takes a hint:
A larger subject may bring down the prize.
He thinks of Thomas Jefferson — but then
Jefferson was a deist, took the Bible

And cut out everything but Jesus' words.
"Yet I can speak on what was good in him,
His work for liberty, the Declaration,
And close my eyes to all his heterodoxy."
Then something of this plan crept like a snake
Into his brain, he petted it with hands:
Be ye as wise as serpents, and as doves
Harmless, he smiled — and went to work again,
And won the prize.

           And now he has stepped forth
Into the world's arena to become
A Savior, an evangel, as he thinks,
In truth a pest.   He runs for Congress first
And when his manager takes out a check
And shows him, given by the local brewery,
Another check a bank gives, he maintains
A smiling silence, thinking to himself,
Jesus accepted gifts from publicans,
And if I am elected then this money,
However dirty, will be purified
By what I do.

           But then he was defeated.
He thinks the banks and breweries did the trick.
In truth they knew the Christian Statesman, knew
The oleaginous smile and silver voice
Concealed the despot.   Did he scourge them then?
Well, scarcely then — he wrote a public letter
And said the people had decided it.

THE CHRISTIAN STATESMAN

And what the people said was law. He nerved
His purpose for another trial — that body
So big and flawless could not be exhausted —
That voice still carried to the farthest corner,
That oily smile deceived the multitude
That he was hurt, embittered, only waited
To see if body, voice and oily smile
Could win by any means; if not, the scourge
Would be brought forth, the smile dropped, the com-
     plaints
Against the breweries, what not, opened up,
Unmasked. For when your hope is gone, you're free
To scold and tell your bitterness.

                              And then
He made a third and last attempt, though edging
Toward the sophistry that moral questions
Make those political, and by this means
Trying to win the churches. Still he stuck
To matters economic, as before
Took what the breweries gave to help his cause,
His campaign fund. By this time many more
Had found him out, and knew him for a voice
And tireless body nourishing a brain
As mediocre as the world contained,
And only making louder noise because
Of body strong and voice mellifluous.
They put him down for good; the Christian Statesman
Had cause to think he was no statesman, or
No Christian, or the electorate not Christian.

And so he took the mask off, dropped the smile,
And let his mouth set like a concrete crack
And went about to punish men, while seeming
To save the world.

                Out of that indentation,
That fosse of mediocrity, came up
A crocodile with wagging tail upreared,
And smile toothed to the gullet — it was this:
Questions political are moral questions,
And moral questions are political,
And terms convertible are equipollent,
And wholly true.   Therefore, I rise to preach
To moral America, draw audiences
In churches, of the churches.   If I win
Majorities upon — no matter what —
A law will blossom; as all moral questions
Are equally political, procure
For their adoption the majority.
Upon this fortress I can stand and shoot —
Who can attack me, since I seek for self
Nothing, but for my country righteousness?
And as an instrument of God I punish
My enemies as well.

                Who are my enemies?
The intelligencia, as they call themselves,
Who flaunt the Bible wholly or in part,
Or try to say that Darwin's evolution
Honors the Deity more than Genesis.

THE CHRISTIAN STATESMAN

Who are my enemies? The thinkers, yes,
The strivers for a higher culture, yes,
The scorners of old fashioned ways, the things
Really American! — I know the crowd —
That smart minority I overwhelm,
Blot out, drown out, by massing under me
The great majority, the common folk,
Believers in the Bible — first for them!
And on the way the vile saloon I crush,
The abominable brewery — then I take away
From banqueters and diners, diners out,
The seekers after happiness, not God,
The cocktail and the wine they love so well.
This is a moral question, being so
Is also a political — the majority
Can do what they desire. I am consistent,
For from the first I've preached the people's rule, ·
Abided by the people's voice and taken
Defeat with grace because the people gave it.
So now I say the people have the right
To pass upon all questions. As I said
When starting as a public man, the people
Could have what Government they desired, in fact
A King, or despotism, if they voted for it.
For all this talk of rights, or realms of right,
Or individual preferences, beliefs
And courses in the world is swallowed up
By right of the majority — the serpent
Of Moses, so to speak, which swallowed up
All other serpents.

STARVED ROCK

If he thought so much
The Christian Statesman thought this way — at least
He acted out a part which seemed to say
He analyzed so far. He went to work
To make his country just a despotism
Not governed by a King, but by the people
Laying the hand of law on everything
Most intimate and private, having thought
For moral aspects, as all politics
Are moral in their essence, to repeat.

Did not the Christian Statesman have revenge
In building his theocracy, who saw
All bills of right and fruit of revolution
Ground into mortar, made into a throne
For Demos?

And behold King Demos now!
A slouch hat for a crown upon his brow,
Stuffed full of bacon and of apple pie,
The Christian Statesman leaning on his shoulder
A tableau of familiarity.
The Christian Statesman having lost his hair
Betrays the Midas ears — the oily smile
Beams on the republic he has overthrown!

THE LAMENT OF SOPHONIA

You who have wasted this June for me,
Bitter be the seed of your love.

Long midnights by the sea
Have I waited for your return,
Counting the stars —
Bitter be the seed of your love.

And as stars go out in the crocus light of dawn,
As waters drip from a failing fountain,
So passed these days of June.
As a boy strips from a stalk of snap-dragons
The perfect blossoms,
And treads them into the earth,
So you have taken the June days from me —
Bitter be the seed of your love.

On my couch by the sea,
My golden curls loosened,
Resting after the cool ablution of evening waters,
My body white as whitecaps, under the moon,
My eyes large as the fox's lurking in darkness,
I have waited for your return.

STARVED ROCK

May the scourge of Asia mar your beautiful body,
Beloved!
You have wasted my loveliest June.
As the unheeding wind
Drives the falling cherry blossoms
Into the purple waves,
So you have scattered my days of June —
Bitter be the seed of your love!

I have distilled henbane for you,
Beloved,
And put it in a crystal vial.
The moon of October will shine,
Then you will come to me,
Your wanderings and treasons finished!
And when you slip exhausted from my arms
I will give you wine from a golden cup,
And pour the henbane in it —
I shall give you henbane for the poison of defeated
    love;
I shall kiss your dead lips, Beloved.

Then I shall drink, too.
Our bodies shall feed the worms
As these June days have fed my writhing sorrow,
Beloved murderer of my June!

AT DECAPOLIS

Mark, Chap. V

I

THE ACCUSATION

I am a farmer and live
Two miles from Decapolis.
Where is the magistrate? Tell me
Where the magistrate is!

Here I had made provision
For children and wife,
And now I have lost my all;
I am ruined for life.

I, a believer, too,
In the synagogues.—
What is the faith to me?
I have lost my hogs.

Two thousand hogs as fine
As ever you saw,
Drowned and choked in the sea —
I want the law!

They were feeding upon a hill
When a strolling teacher

Came by and scared my hogs —
They say he's a preacher,

And cures the possessed who haunt
The tombs and bogs.
All right; but why send devils
Into my hogs?

They squealed and grunted and ran
And plunged in the sea.
And the lunatic laughed who was healed,
Of the devils free.

Devils or fright, no matter
A fig or straw.
Where is the magistrate, tell me —
I want the law!

II

JESUS BEFORE MAGISTRATE AHAZ

Ahaz, there in the seat of judgment, hear,
  If you have wit to understand my plea.
Swine-devils are too much for swine, that's clear,
  Poor man possessed of such is partly free,

Is neither drowned, destroyed at once, his chains
  May pluck while running, howling through the mire
And take a little gladness for his pains,
  Some fury for unsatisfied desire.

[80]

AT DECAPOLIS

But hogs go mad at once.   All this I knew,—
   But then this lunatic had rights.   You grant
Swine-devils had him in their clutch and drew
   His baffled spirit.   How significant,

As they were legion and so named, the point
   Is, life bewildered, torn in greed and wrath.
Desire puts a spirit out of joint.
   Swine-devils are for swine, who have no path.

But man with many lusts, what is his way,
   Save in confusion, through accustomed rooms?
He prays for night to come, and for the day
   Amid the miry places and the tombs.

But hogs run to the sea.   And there's an end.
   Would I might cast the swinish demons out
From man forever.   Yet the word attend.
   The lesson of the thing what soul can doubt?

What is the loss of hogs, if man be saved?
   What loss of lands and houses, man being free?
Clothed in his reason sits the man who raved,
   Clean and at peace, your honor.   Come and see.

Your honor shakes a frowning head.   Not loth,
   Speaking more plainly, deeper truth to draw;
Do your judicial duty, yet I clothe
   Free souls with courage to transgress the law

STARVED ROCK

By casting demons out from self, or those
  Like this poor lunatic whom your synagogues
Would leave to battle singly with his woes —
  What is a man's soul to a drove of hogs?

Which being lost, men play the hypocrite
  And make the owner chief in the affair.
You banish me for witchcraft. I submit.
  Work of this kind awaits me everywhere.

And into swine where better they belong,
Casting the swinish devils out of men
The devils have their place at last, and then
  The man is healed who had them — where's the wrong

Save to the owner? Well, your synagogues
  Make the split hoof and chewing of the cud
The test of lawful flesh. Not so are hogs.
  This rule has been the statute from the flood.

Ahaz, your judgment has a fatal flaw.
  Is it not so with judges first and last —
You break the law to specialize the law? —
  This is the devil that from you I cast.

WINGED VICTORY

Icarus, Daedalus, Medea's dragons,
Pegasus, Leonardo, Swedenborg,
Cyrano de Bergerac, with dew-filled flagons,
Bacon, who schemed with chemicals and forge,
Lana, of copper spheres of air exhausted,
Therefore made light to rise
Up where the pathless ways are frosted
In the blue vitriol of the skies.

Montgolfier, Franklin, von Zeppelin, Watt,
Edison, an engine must be, spiral springs,
Nor steam move not these more than condor wings
Of heaven's Argonaut,
Gathering the sun-set clouds for golden fleece.
Santos Dumont and Langley, over these
The Americans, the brothers Wright.
America finds wings for flight.
At last out of the New World wings are born
To wheel far up where cold is, and a light
Dazzling and immaculate,
In the heights where stands the temple of the Morn.
Winged Victory more beautiful than Samothrace's
For the New World opening the gate
Of heaven at last, where mortals enter in
Unconquerably and win

STARVED ROCK

The great escape from earth, the measureless spaces
Of air across the inimical abyss
Between ethereal precipice and precipice.
Hail! spirits of the race's
Courage to be free, adventurers
Of infinite desire!
Hail! seed of the ancient wars,
Of burning glasses, catapults, Greek fire!
Hail! final conquerors,
Out of whose vision greater vision springs —
America with wings!

The vulture lags behind, the Gorgones,
Revealed or ambushed in the thunder clouds,
Would tear from heaven these audacities
Of deathless spirit, shatter them and spill
The blasphemy of genius from the sky.
Gods are you, flyers, whom no danger shrouds,
No terror shakes the will.
Gods are you though you suffer and must die,
Men winged as gods who fly!

Borelli, in the centuries that are gone,
With feathers made him wings, but steel
Soars for the petrol demon's toil,
Fed by the sap of trees far under earth
In the long eons past turned into oil.
The petrol demon in the enchanted coil
Of lightning howls and spins the invisible wheel
Which had its birth

WINGED VICTORY

In the rapt vision of Archimides.
Borelli, in the centuries that are gone,
With feathers made him wings. But now a swan,
A steel-borne beetle cleaves the immensities,
Fed with fire of amber and oil of trees,
And soars against the sun,
And over mountains, seas!

Flight more auspicious than the flight of cranes
In Homer's Troyland, or than eagles flying
Toward Imaus when the midnight wanes.
Victorious flight! symbol of man defying
Low dungeons of the spirit, darkness, chains.
Flight beyond superstition and the reigns
Of tyrannies where thought of man should be
Swift as his thought is free.
Flight of an era born to-day
That puts the past and all its dead away.

Locusts of the new Jehovah sent to scourge
All Pharaohs who enslave.
Hornets with multiple eyes,
Scorning surprise,
And armed to purge
The despot and the knave
Out of the fairer land where men shall live,
Winning all things which were so fugitive
Of wisdom, happiness and peace,
Of hope, of spiritual release

STARVED ROCK

From fear of life, life's mean significance,
Till life be ordered, not a thing of chance.

The hopelessness of him who cried
Vanity of Vanities
Was justified,
But now no longer must abide.
Failure was his, and failure filled the hours
Of our fathers in the past — let it depart.
Triumph is come, and triumph must be ours.
The archangels of earth through Israel,
Through India and Greece
Shall find us wings for life and for increase
Of living, and shall battle down the hell
Whose fires still smolder and profane.
Life and the human heart
In living must become the aeroplane,
Not the yoked oxen and the cart.
Let but the thought of East and West be blent,
Europe, America, the Orient,
To give life wings as Time's last great event:
The final glory of wings to the soul of man
In an order of life human, but divine,
Fashioned in carefulest thought, powerful but of delicate
    design,
As the wings of the aeroplane are.
Where spirit of man is used to the full, but saved,
As the petrol demon, in this dragon of war,
Uses and saves his power.

WINGED VICTORY

Where neither thought, truth, love nor gifts, nor any
    flower
Of spirit of man, so mangled or enslaved
In the eras gone, is wasted or depraved.

Man shall no longer crawl, the curse is raised
With winning of his wings.
Dust he no more shall eat,
Who crawls not, but from feet
Has risen to wings!
Man shall no longer python be.
These wings are prophecies of a world made free!
Man shall no longer crawl, the curse is raised.
He has soared to the gate of heaven and gazed
Into the meadows of infinity,
Winged and with lightning shod,
Beyond the old day's lowering cloud and murk.
The heavens declare the glory of God,
Man shows His handiwork!

OH YOU SABBATARIANS!

Oh you sabbatarians, methodists and puritans;
You bigots, devotees and ranters;
You formalists, pietists and fanatics,
Teetotalers and hydropots,
You thin ascetics, androgynous souls,
Chaste and epicene spirits,
Eyes blind to color, ears deaf to sound,
Fingers insensitive,
Do what you will,
Make what laws you choose —
Yet there are high spaces of rapture
Which you can never touch,
They are beyond you and hidden from you.

We leave you to the dull assemblies,
Charades, cantatas and lectures;
The civic meetings where you lie and act
And work up business;
The teas of forced conversation,
And receptions of how-de-dos,
And stereotyped smiles;
The church sociables;
And the calls your young men of clammy hands
And fetid breath
Pay to anæmic virgins —

OH YOU SABBATARIANS!

These are yours;
Take them —
But I tell you
In places you know not of,
We, the free spirits, the livers,
Guests at the wedding feast of life,
Drinkers of the wine made by Jesus,
Worshipers of fire and of God,
Who made the grape,
And filled the veins of His legitimate children
With ethereal flame —
We the lovers of life in unknown places
Shall taste of ancient wine,
And put flowers in golden vases,
And open precious books of song,
And look upon dreaming Buddhas,
And marble masks of genius.
We shall hear the sound of stringed instruments,
Voicing the dreams of great spirits.
We shall know the rapture of kisses
And long embraces,
And the sting of folly.
We shall entwine our arms in voluptuous sleep,
And in the misery of your denials
And your cowardice and your fears
You shall not even dream that we exist.

Unintelligible weeds! We, the blossoms of life's garden,
Flourish on the hills of variable winds —
We perish, but you never live.

PALLAS ATHENE

Athene! Virgin! Goddess! Queen! descend,
Come to us and befriend.
Set up your shrine among us and defend
Our realm against corruptions which impend.

*   *   *   *   *

Divinity of order and of law,
Most powerful and wise,
Our land reclaim.
Patron of the assemblies of the free,
Our cities shame!
Dethrone our bastard Demos, partisans
Of Moody, Campbell, all the Wesleyans.
Come down with awe,
Enceladus and Pallas strike, who rise
Against your father and his hierarchy.
Smite the giants Superstition, Force,
Fanaticism, Ignorance and Faith
In village gods, and bury them beneath
Volcanic mountains.   Yoke them to the course
And labor of your wisdom.   Fling your shield,
Medusa faced, before the brows of clay,
Who rule our clattering day;
Flash it before their brows and make
Stones for the pavement of the way

PALLAS ATHENE

Whereon you drive your chariot, golden-wheeled.
Descend, O Goddess, for the memory's sake
And for the hope's sake of your son,
Franklin, your herald, Washington,
Who dreamed to make perpetual
Our Parthenon, column, court and hall.
And save it from the donjon, minaret,
The cross, the spire, the vane, the parapet!

*   *   *   *   *

We have no god but Jesus,
No god but Billiken.
Nature and Dionysius
Come back again!
Jehovah is an alien tyrant, rules us
From arid Palestine,
Who mouths a heaven that fools us,
And curses the olive and vine,
And the smiles of the lyric nine.
Gods are they, hard and full of wrath
Who drive us on the unintelligible path.
Gods are they, and unreckoning of their work
Too puerile or despotic, or with feet
That drip blood on a mercy seat.
They nerve our hands with hatred's dirk,
Or weaken us with poison sweet.
Drug us to mumble this is life, who feel
In our delirium, no less, that life
Is an ocean that breaks the grist stones and the wheel
Set up to feed this world of strife

[91]

STARVED ROCK

By Mary's son, Mary the wife ——
Come from the Islands of the Blest,
Goddess, and give us wisdom, vision, rest.
Reveal a Beauty for our hearts to love.
The wooden ark of Moses, overlaid
With strips of gold,
And all the spurious covenant thereof
By which our life is obelised
We would no more behold,
Who have so vainly with it temporized.
Fruitless our spirits have these centuries prayed
Before the Janus cross,
The oracle that speaks in riddles, asks
Penitence, obedience, tasks
Which nature interdicts.
We are the body on the crucifix,
Not Jesus; we, the race, are crucified,
And die upon the cross,
For centuries have died.
Come and restore our loss
Of truth, the eyes of spirits undeceived,
Courage with nature, strike the opiate joss
To ruin with your sword,
O most adored!
Give us Reality, O lover of men,
Republics, cities, lands.
Uplift our eyes to Beauty, once perceived
We may rebuild the Areopagus,
With wiser eyes and hands.
Bring Thought, the Argus, consciousness

PALLAS ATHENE

That looks before and after,
And grace perpetual of Mnemosyne —
Remembering we shall be free!
Save us, O Goddess, from the drifting crowd,
Wondering, witless, loud,
The lovers of the minute who possess
No reverence and no laughter!

* * * * *

Goddess! with silver helmet, guardian
You may be, if we worship at your shrine,
Before the gates of Boston and New York,
Chicago, San Francisco, through the span
Of continents and isles; your heart incline
Toward our turbulent blood from many climes,
Worships and times.
Lift from our necks the brass and jeweled torque
Of restless zealots and of idiot mouths;
The locusts swarm, the land is cursed with drouths,
Bring rain and dew,
Plant olive trees,
Set on our hills the emblem of the vine;
Bring to our hearts the lofty purities
Of song and laughter, wisdom, and renew
Temples of beauty and academies!

* * * * *

Set up your golden altar
In Parthenons in every village and shire.
The crucifix and psalter,
The ikons and the toys of vain desire

STARVED ROCK

We cast into the fire.
We keep the lover Jesus, for his hope,
His humanism and his flaming zeal.
He will approach your altar, he will kneel
At last before you, for the horoscope
Of life misread in youth
And youthful dreams and faith.
Goddess! our globe that hungers for the truth
Between the roar of life, silence of death
Cannot be stayed or cowed. But, oh, descend
First to our soil, Atlantis, and befriend.
Make us a light across the fathomless sea
Of centuries to be,
Even as Athens is, divinity!

AT SAGAMORE HILL

All things proceed as though the stage were set
For acts arranged. I have not learned the part,
The day enacts itself. I take the tube,
Find daylight at Jamaica, know the place
Through some rehearsal, all the country know
Which glides along the window, is not seen
For definite memory. At Oyster Bay
A taxi stands in readiness; in a trice
We circle strips of water, slopes of hills,
Climb where a granite wall supports a hill,
A mass of blossoms, ripening berries, too,
And enter at a gate, go up a drive,
Shadowed by larches, cedars, silver willows.
This taxi just ahead is in the play,
Is here in life as I had seen it in
The crystal of prevision, reaches first
The porte cochere. This moment from the door
Comes Roosevelt, and greets the man who leaves
The taxi just ahead, then waits for me,
Puts a strong hand that softens into mine,
And says, O, this is bully!

                              We go in.
He leaves my antecessor in a room
Somewhere along the hall, and comes to me

STARVED ROCK

Who wait him in the roomy library.
How are those lovely daughters? Oh, by George!
I thought I might forget their names, I know —
It's Madeline and Marcia. Yes, you know
Corinne adores the picture which you sent
Of Madeline — your boy, too? In the war!
That's bully — tea is coming — we must talk,
I have five hundred things to ask you — set
The tea things on this table, Anna — now,
Do you take sugar, lemon? O, you smoke!
I'll give you a cigar.

                            The talk begins.
He's dressed in canvas khaki, flannel shirt,
Laced boots for farming, chopping trees, perhaps;
A stocky frame, curtains of skin on cheeks
Drained slightly of their fat; gash in the neck
Where pus was emptied lately; one eye dim,
And growing dimmer; almost blind in that.
And when he walks he rolls a little like
A man whose youth is fading, like a cart
That rolls when springs are old. He is a moose,
Scarred, battered from the hunters, thickets, stones;
Some finest tips of antlers broken off,
And eyes where images of ancient things
Flit back and forth across them, keeping still
A certain slumberous indifference
Or wisdom, it may be.

AT SAGAMORE HILL

But then the talk!
Bronze dolphins in a fountain cannot spout
More streams at once: Of course the war, the emperor,
America in the war, his sons in France,
The dangers, separation, let them go!
The fate has been appointed — to our task,
Live full our lives with duty, go to sleep!
For I say, he exclaims, the man who fears
To die should not be born, nor left to live.
It's Celtic poetry, free verse. He says:
You nobly celebrate in your Spoon River
The pioneers, the soldiers of the past,
Why do you flout our Philippine adventure?
No difference, Colonel, in the stock, the difference
Lies in the causes. Well, another stream:
Mark Hanna, Quay and others, what I hate,
He says to me, is the Pharisee — I can stand
All other men. And you will find the men
So much maligned had gentle qualities,
And noble dreams. Poor Quay, he loved the Indians,
Sent for me when he lay there dying, said,
Look after such a tribe when I am dead.
I want to crawl upon a sunny rock
And die there like a wolf. Did he say that,
Colonel, to you? Yes! and you know, a man
Who says a thing like that has in his soul
An orb of light to flash that meaning forth
Of heroism, nature.

Time goes on,
The play is staged, must end; my taxi comes

STARVED ROCK

In half an hour or so. Before it comes,
Let's walk about the farm and see my corn.
A fellow on the porch is warming heels
As we go by. I'll see him when you go,
The Colonel says.

           The rail fence by the corn
Is good to lean on as we stand and talk
Of farming, cattle, country life. We turn,
Sit for some moments in a garden house
On which a rose vine clambers all in bloom,
And from this hilly place look at the strips
Of water from the bay a mile beyond,
Below some several terraces of hills
Where firs and pines are growing. This resembles
A scene in Milton that I've read. He knows,
Catches the reminiscence, quotes the lines — and then
Something of country silence, look of grass
Where the wind stirs it, mystical little breaths
Coming between the roses; something, too,
In Vulcan's figure; he is Vulcan, too,
Deprived his shop, great bellows, hammer, anvil,
Sitting so quietly beside me, hands
Spread over knees; something of these evokes
A pathos, and immediately in key
With all of this he says: I have achieved
By labor, concentration, not at all
By gifts or genius, being commonplace
In all my faculties.

AT SAGAMORE HILL

                              Not all, I say.
One faculty is not, your over-mind,
Eyed front and back to see all faculties,
Govern and watch them.   If we let you state
Your case against you, timid born, you say,
Becoming brave, asthmatic, growing strong:
No marksman, yet becoming skilled with guns;
No gift of speech, yet winning golden speech;
No gift of writing, writing books, no less
Of our America to thrill and live —
If, as I say, we let you state your case
Against you as you do, there yet remains
This over-mind, and that is what — a gift
Of genius or of what?   By George, he says,
What are you, a theosophist?   I don't know.
I know some men achieve a single thing,
Like courage, charity, in this incarnation;
You have achieved some twenty things.   I think
That this is going some for a man whose gifts
Are commonplace and nothing else.

                              We rise
And saunter toward the house — and there's the man
Still warming heels; my taxi, too, has come.
We are to meet next Wednesday in New York
And finish up some subjects — he has thoughts
How I can help America, if I drop
This line or that a little, all in all.

        *   *   *   *   *

STARVED ROCK

But something happens; I have met a loss;
Would see no one, and write him I am off.
And on that Wednesday flashes from the war
Say Quentin has been killed: we had not met
If I had stayed to meet him.

                                    So, good-by
Upon the lawn at Sagamore was good-by,
Master of Properties, you stage the scene
And let us speak and pass into the wings!
One thing was fitting — dying in your sleep —
A touch of Nature, Colonel, you who loved
And were beloved of Nature, felt her hand
Upon your brow at last to give to you
A bit of sleep, and after sleep perhaps
Rest and rejuvenation; you will wake
To newer labors, fresher victories
Over those faculties not disciplined
As you desired them in these sixty years.

TO ROBERT NICHOLS

England has found another voice in you
   Of beauty and of truth,
True to their soul, as you are true —
   Singer and soldier, yet a youth.

Out of the trenches and the rage of blood,
   The hatred and the lies
You, like a wounded sky-lark, in a flood
   Pour forth these melodies,

Of a spirit which has suffered, yet has soared
   Above the stench of hell and death's defeats.
I look at you, as often I have pored
   On the death mask of Keats.

Or the face of him quickly and gladly going
   The waves of the sea under,
To the land of man's unknowing,
   Or the land of wonder.

And the war had you! what can it give
   In return for souls like yours
Mangled or blotted out? — who shall forgive
   The war while time endures?

STARVED ROCK

Back of the shouting mob, the brazen bands,
   The soldiers marching well,
Gangrene cries out and Rupert Brooke's hands
   Clutch in a hemorrhage of hell.

Yet you found God through this? through war,
   Through love found vision, perhaps peace?
Keep them in your breast like the morning star —
   May their light increase.

Waves on the sea's breast catch the light
   While the hollows between
Are dark — you are a wave whose height
   Is smitten by the Light unseen,

Urged by the Sea's power to the glory
   Of the christening sun.
When the calm comes and darkness, transitory
   Be your doubt, or none.

These words from me who have the hard way traveled
   Of pain and thought,
In a weaving never wholly unraveled,
   Or wholly wrought,

For your spirit and your songs, gladness
   For the hope of you, and praise
To life, who gave you out of the world's madness
   In these our days.

BONNYBELL: THE BUTTERFLY

As I shall die, let your belief
Find in these words too poor and brief
My soul's essential self.

                         My grief
Down to the day I knew you locks
Its secret word in paradox:
I who loved truth could not be true,
Could only love the truth and glow
With words of truth who loved it so,
Even while I dishonored you.
I who loved constancy was false,
And heeded but in part the calls
Of loveliness for love and you.
I am but half of that I hoped,
And that half hardly more than words
I cheered my soul with as it groped:
As from their bowers of rain the birds
Sing feebly, pining for the sun.
As I am all of this, by fate
Lose what I could so well have won,
Life leaves me half articulate,
My failure, nature half-expressed,
Or wholly hidden in my breast.
Yes, dear, the secret of me lies

STARVED ROCK

Where words scarce come to analyze.
Yet who knows why he is this or that?
What moves, defeats him, works him ill?
What blood ancestral of the bat
Narrows his music to the shrill
Squeak of a flitting thing that hunts
For gnats, which never singing, fronts
The full moon flooding down the vale,
The perfect soul, the nightingale!

You have wooed music all your life,
And I have sought for love. I think
My soul was marked, dear, by a wife
Who loved a man immersed in drink,
Who crushed her love which would not **die.**
If this be true, my soul's great thirst
Was blended with a fault accursed.
My mother's love is my soul's cry.
My father's vileness, lies and lusts,
His cruel heart, inconstancy
That kept my mother with the crusts
Of life to gnaw, are in my blood.
My rainbow wings I scarce can **loose,**
Or if I free them, there's the mud
That weighs and mars their use.

You have wooed music. But suppose
The hampered hours and poverty
Broke down your spirit's harmony,
Then if you found you could achieve

BONNYBELL: THE BUTTERFLY

The music in you, if you could
But pick a pocket or deceive,
Which would you call the greater good —
The music or a sin withstood?
Suppose you passed a window where
The violin of your despair
Lay ready for your hands! At last
You stole it as you hurried past,
And hid it underneath your rags
Until you reached your attic room,
Then tuned the strings and burned the tags.
And drew the bow till lyric fire
Should all your thieving thoughts consume:
In such case what is your desire —
The music or the violin?
And what in such case is your sin?
And if they caught you in your theft,
Would you, just to be honest, dear,
Forefront your thief-self as your deft
And dominant genius, or the ear
Which tortured you?

                Would you not say,
Music intrigues me night and day?
My soul is the musician's.   First
In my soul's love is music.   Would
You falsify to keep your good?
Deny your theft, or put the worst
Construction on your soul, obscure
Thereby your soul's investiture

STARVED ROCK

Of music's gift and music's lure?
If you were flame you would pretend
What you would fain be to the end,
Keep your good name and keep as well
The violin.   May this not be
In some realm an integrity?

Now for myself, dear, though I lack
The gift of utterance to explain
My life's pursuit and passion, pain,
Or why I acted thus, concealed
Thoughts that you hold were best revealed,
Your eyes to heal themselves must track
And find my soul's way in its quest
Followed from girlhood without rest.
Music is not its hope, but love. . . .
And I saw somehow I could lift
My life through you, and rise above
What I had been.   And since your gift
Of love saw me as truthful, true
I kept that best side to your view,
And hoped to be what you desired
If I but struggled, still aspired.
And as for lapses, even while
I fooled you with the wanton's smile,
He was my lover till you came
To light my life with purer flame.
Was it, beloved, so great a sin?
He was a practice violin.
Oh, how I knew this when your strings

BONNYBELL: THE BUTTERFLY

Sang to me afterward when I slept
Upon your breast again. I wept,
Do you remember? I was grieving
Neither for him, nor your deceiving,
Rather (how strange is life) that he
Was prelude to your harmony;
Rather that while I walked with him,
With you I found the cherubim,
Left my old self at last with wings,
Saw beauty clear where it was dim
Before through my imaginings.

Do you suppose the primrose knows
What skill adds petals to its crown?
How many failures laugh and frown
Upon the hand that crosses, sows?
The hand is ignorant of the power
Obedient in the primrose flower
To the hand's skill that toils to add
New petals till the flower be clad
In fuller glory. What's the bond
Between us two, that I respond
To what you are?   Nor do you know
What lies within me fain to grow
Under your hand.

                    But if the worm
Should call itself the butterfly,
Since it will soon become one, I
Better to be myself affirm

STARVED ROCK

'That I am Beauty, Truth — for you
I would be Beauty, Truth, imbue
Your life with love and loveliness.
And you can make me Beauty, Truth,
And I can bring you soul success
If you but train my flower whose youth
Still may be governed, keep erect
My hope in this poor earthen sod.
I think this is a task which God
Appoints for us. We may neglect
The task in this life, but to find
It is a task we leave behind,
Only to meet it, till we see
Our fate worked out in lives to be.

O, from my lesser self to spread
My golden wings above your head,
Through love of love and you discard
The sting, the rings of green, the shard.
Oh, to be Psyche, passion tried
Through flesh, desire, purified!
Love is my lode-star, music yours —
Souls must go where the lode-star lures.

HYMN TO AGNI

God of fire,
God of the flame of our love,
Beyond whose might no God is,
And none in the realm of birth,
Agni!   Adored one,
May we never suffer in thy friendship!

Thou, who art re-born each day,
And whose symbol is the sacred drill
Wherewith fire is made for the temple,
Morning by morning,
Freshly create our love as the sun awakes,
Preserve our love, O Agni!

The crocuses, the dandelions,
The golden forsythia
Perished in May.
But roses burn on the altar of earth,
Bridal blossoms, whitest of fire,
Dance in the winds of June.
Agni, remember us,
Remember our love!

We have prayed to you, powerful one —
Thou whose name is first

STARVED ROCK

In the first of the sacred hymns;
Thou to whom sacrifices pass
To the Gods, thou messenger of the Gods,
Thou who art born a little lower than the most
    high Indra
Hast heard our prayer —
Hear still our prayer:
Abide with us, O Agni, and befriend;
Make our hearts as temples,
And our desire as the drill,
Wherewith fire is created
For the sacred sacrifice of love,
And for a light to our spirits —
Turn not away from our prayers,
O Agni!

Here before the fire of the Sun of June
Kneeling
Hand in hand,
Our eyes closed before the splendor of your spirit
Hear our prayer, O Agni:
May we never suffer in thy friendship.

EPITAPH FOR US

One with the turf, one with the tree
As we are now, you soon shall be,
As you are now, so once were we.

The hundred years we looked upon
Were Goethe and Napoleon.
Now twice a hundred years are gone,

And you gaze back and contemplate,
Lloyd George and Wilson, William's hate,
And Nicholas of the bloody fate;

Us, too, who won the German war,
Who knew less what the strife was for
Than you, now that the conqueror

Lies with the conquered.   You will say:
" Here sleep the brave, the grave, the gay,
The wise, the blind, who lost the way."

But for us English, for us French,
Americans who held the trench,
You will not grieve, though the rains drench

STARVED ROCK

The hills and valleys, being these.
Who pities stocks, or pities trees?
Or stones, or meadows, rivers, seas?

We are with nature, we have grown
At one with water, earth, and stone —
Man only is separate and alone,

Earth sundered, left to dream and feel
Illusion still in pain made real,
The hope a mist, but fire the wheel.

But what was love, and what was lust,
Memory, passion, pain or trust,
Returned to clay and blown in dust,

Is nature without memory —
Yet as you are, so once were we,
As we are now, you soon shall be,

Blind fellows of the indifferent stars
Healed of your bruises, of your scars
In love and living, in the wars.

Come to us where the secret lies
Under the riddle of the skies,
Surrender fingers, speech, and eyes.

Sink into nature and become
The mystery that strikes you dumb,
Be clay and end your martyrdom.

EPITAPH FOR US

Rise up as thought, the secret know.
As passionless as stars bestow
Your glances on the world below,

As a man looks at hand or knee.
What is the turf of you, what the tree?
Earth is a phantom — let it be.

BOTTICELLI TO SIMONETTA

I would give you all my heart, and I have given
    All my heart to you to have and keep
With your heart, where my heart has found its heaven
    In a light immortal, and a peace like sleep.
Here is my heart, for you to have and treasure,
    Your woman's heart will treasure it,
For a love that only love may find a measure,
    And only love like yours can measure it.

In absence and in separation praying
    Before your love, my heart receive,
My heart which kneels to you, so gently laying
    Hands of deep prayer, too reverent to grieve
For lives divided, yet compassionate,
    As my poor heart is pitiful for yours.
These hearts of ours, that know so deep a fate,
    Even as a heart that silently endures,
Lie on an altar of consuming fire,
    Our hearts together, taking life thereof.
Ashes must come of two hearts which aspire
    To God, who has given love.

FLOWER IN THE GARDEN

Flower in the garden,
Wholly itself and free,
Yearning and joyous,
Breathing its charm
To the passer-by
On the sighing air —
Beloved flower!
Flower desired for something beyond
Itself as a flower;
Giving the promise of ecstasy
Beyond its own being,
Its place in the garden —
A shadowed flame
Of an absolute!

Flower that I have taken
From its place in the garden
To realize the ultimate Beauty;
Flower in the vase at my side,
Breathing a sweeter life
Into the air I breathe,
A spirit that makes me faint,
Sorrowful with a strange languor.
Flower no less beautiful,
But revealing an essence

[115]

That changes my flower.
O, my flower that is with me but lost,
Lost in the disclosure of other hues,
Other scents!

Flower of passion, flower of love,
Flower that I have won and lost,
Mystical flower!

INEXORABLE DEITIES

Deities!
Inexorable revealers,
Give me strength to endure
The gifts of the Muses,
Daughters of Memory.
When the sky is blue as Minerva's eyes
Let me stand unshaken;
When the sea sings to the rising sun
Let me be unafraid;
When the meadow lark falls like a meteor
Through the light of afternoon,
An unloosened fountain of rapture,
Keep my heart from spilling
Its vital power;
When at the dawn
The dim souls of crocuses hear the calls
Of waking birds,
Give me to live but master the loveliness.
Keep my eyes unharmed from splendors
Unveiled by you,
And my ears at peace
Filled no less with the music
Of Passion and Pain, growth and change.

  *   *   *   *   *

STARVED ROCK

But O ye sacred and terrible powers,
Reckless of my mortality,
Strengthen me to behold a face,
To know the spirit of a beloved one
Yet to endure, yet to dare!

ARIELLE

Arielle! Arielle!
Gracious and fanciful,
Laughing and joyous!
Arielle girlish, queenly, majestical;
Deep eyed for memory,
Pensive for dreams.
Arielle crowned with the light of thought,
Mystical, reverent,
Musing on the splendor of life,
And the blossom of love
Pressed into her hands —
Arielle!

Music awakes in the hall!
Shadowy pools and glistening willows,
And elfin shapes amid silver shadows
Are made into sound!
Arielle listens with hidden eyes,
Sitting amid her treasures,
A presence like a lamp of alabaster,
A yearning gardenia
That broods in a shaft of light . . .
Arielle clapping hands and running
About her rooms,
Arranging cloths of gold and jars of crystal,

And vases of ruby cloisonne.
Arielle matching blues and reds:
Pomegranates, apples in bowls of jade.
Arielle reposing, lost in Plato,
In the contemplation of Agni.
Arielle, the cup to her lips,
A laughing Thalia!
Arielle!

The breath of morning moves through the casement
     window —
Arielle taking the cool of it on her brow,
And the ecstasy of the robin's song into her heart.
Arielle in prayer at dawn
Laying hands upon secret powers:
Lead me in the path of love to my love.
Arielle merging the past and the present,
As light increases light —
Arielle adored —
Arielle!

SOUNDS OUT OF SORROW

Of all sounds out of the soul of sorrow
These I would hear no more:
The cry of a new-born child at midnight;
The sound of a closing door,

That hushes the echo of departing feet
When the loneliness of the room
Is haunted with the silence
Of a dead god's tomb;

The songs of robins at the white dawn,
Since I may never see
The eyes they waked in the April
Now gone from me;

Music into whose essence entered
The soul of an hour: —
A face, a voice, the touch of a hand,
The scent of a flower.

MOURNIN' FOR RELIGION

Brothers and sisters, I'm mournin' for religion,
But I can't get religion, it's my woman interferin'.
I sing and I pray, and I'm real perseverin,'
But I can't get religion,
That's all I have to say.
I know there is a fountain, a Jesus, a comforter,
A heaven, a Jerusalem, a day of Pentecost,
Salvation for the wishin', blood for sin's remission,
A covenant, a promise for souls that are lost.
But I can't get religion, the salvation feelin',
The vision of the Lamb, forgiveness and healin'.
I have a sort of numbness
When I see the mourners kneelin'.
I have a kind of dumbness
When the preacher is appealin'.
I have a kind of wariness, even contrariness,
Even while I'm fearin'
The bottomless pit and the shut gates of heaven.
It's my woman interferin'—

For you see when they say:
Come to the mercy seat, come, come,
The spirit and the bride
Say come, come,

MOURNIN' FOR RELIGION

I think of my woman who bore so many children;
I think of her a cookin' for harvesters in summer;
I think of her a lyin' there, a dyin' there, the neighbors
Who came in to fan her and how she never murmured;
And then I seem to grow number and number,
And something in me says:
Why didn't Jesus help her for to die,
Why did Jesus always pass her by,
Let her break her health down as I was growing poorer,
Let her lie and suffer with no medicine to cure her,
I wouldn't treat a stray dog as Jesus acted to her.
If these are devil words, I'm a child of the devil.
And this is why I'm dumb
As the spirit and the bride say come!

*   *   *   *   *

I am old and crippled — sixty in December.
And I wonder if it's God that stretches out and hands us
Troubles we remember?
I'm alone besides, I need the Comforter,
All the children's grown up, livin' out in Kansas.
My old friend Billy died of lung fever. . . .
But the worst of it is I'm really a believer,
Expect to go to hell if I don't get religion.
And I need this religion to stop this awful grievin'
About my woman lyin' there in the cemetery,
And you can't stop that grievin' simply by believin'.
So I mourn for religion,
I mourn for religion,
My old heart breaks for religion!

THYAMIS

Thyamis, a gallant of Memphis,
Where melons were served
Iced with snow from the Mountains of the Moon;
Thyamis, a philanderer in Alexandris
Rich in parchments and terebinth,
Lies here in the museum.
His lips are brown as peach leather,
Through which his teeth are sticking,
White as squash seeds.

     *   *   *   *   *

Knowing that he must die and leave her
He slew the lovely Chariclea
Who sailed with him on the Nile
Under the moon of Egypt.
This is the body of Chariclea
Undesiring the arms of Thyamis.
This is the remnant of Chariclea,
Wrapped in a gunny sack,
Rotted with gums and balsams.

     *   *   *   *   *

As the sands of the desert are stirred
By the wind when the sun sets,
The open door of the museum
Lets in the wind to shake

THYAMIS

The cerements of Chariclea,
And the stray hairs on the forsaken head
Of Thyamis.

*   *   *   *   *

Of desire long dead;
Of a murder done in the days of Pharaoh;
Of Thyamis dying who took to death
The lovely Chariclea;
Of Chariclea who shrank
From the love death of Thyamis
The multitude passes, unknowing.

*   *   *   *   *

I SHALL GO DOWN INTO THIS LAND

I shall go down into this land
Of the great Northwest:
This land of the free ordinance,
This land made free for the free
By the patriarchs.

*   *   *   *   *

Shall it be Michigan,
Or Illinois,
Or Indiana?
These are my people,
These are my lovers, my friends —
Mingle my dust with theirs,
Ye sacred powers!

*   *   *   *   *

Clouds, like convoys on infinite missions,
Bound for infinite harbors
Float over the length of this land.
And in the centuries to come
The rocks and trees of this land will turn,
These fields and hills will turn
Under unending convoys of clouds —
O ye clouds!
Drench my dust and mingle it
With the dust of the pioneers;

I SHALL GO DOWN INTO THIS LAND

My mates, my friends,
Toilers and sufferers,
Builders and dreamers,
Lovers of freedom.

  *   *   *   *   ✱

O Earth that looks into space,
As a man in sleep looks up,
And is voiceless, at peace,
Divining the secret —
I shall know the secret
When I go down into this land
Of the great Northwest!

  *   *   *   *   ✱

Draw my dust
With the dust of my beloved
Into the substance of a great rock,
Upon whose point a planet flames,
Nightly, in a thrilling moment
Of divine revelation
Through endless time!

SPRING LAKE

Βῆ δε' κατ' Ουλύμπιο καρήνων χωομενυς κῆρ.
— *Iliad.*

I

Some thought a bomb hit
Trotter's garage.
Some thought a comet
Blew up the Lodge.
Milem Alkire was riding in a Dodge,
Saw the water splashing, and a great light flashing,
And a thousand arrows flying from the heaven's glow;
And heard a great banging and a howling clanging
Of a bull-hide's string to a monstrous bow.

II

Milem Alkire became a changed man,
So the thing began, guess it if you can.
He turned in an hour from a man who was sour
To a singing, dancing satyr like Pan.
He hobbled and clattered as if nothing mattered
Down in his cellar for any strange fellow,
Bringing up the bottles, clinking, winking,
For the crowd that was drinking.
All against the statutes in such case provided.

[128]

SPRING LAKE

Drew well water to cool the wine off,
Polished up the glasses with a humorous cough.
Milem Alkire for years had resided
A quiet, pious, law abiding citizen
Turned in an hour to a wag who derided
The feelings of the people, the village steeple,
And the ways that befit a man —
This Spring Lake citizen.

III

And about the time
That Milem Alkire
Became a wine seller,
And begetter of crime,
With parties on his lawn
From mid-night to dawn,
Making the wine free
Under the pine tree,
Starling Turner's wife ran away,
A woman who before was anything but gay.
Never had a lover in her life, so they say,
But like other clay, had the longing to stray.
She saw a cornet player,
An idler, a strayer,
And left her husband furious threatening to slay her,
And cursing musicians who have no honest missions.
So Starling Turner, a belated learner
Of life as music, laughter, folly,
Grew suddenly jolly, forgot his melancholy,

Became a dancer and rounded up the fiddlers,
Got up a contest of fifty old fiddlers,
With prizes for fiddling from best to middling:
A set of fine harness for the best piece of fiddling.
Work stopped, business stopped, all went mad,
Mad about music, the preachers looked sad
For music, the like of which the village never had. . . .
The children in the street were shockingly bad,
And danced like pixies scantily clad;
Knocked away the crutches from venerable hobblers,
Threw pebbles at the windows of grocers and cobblers,
Made fun of the preachers, the grammar school teachers,
Stole spring chickens and turkey gobblers,
Roasted hooked geese in front of the police.
Till the quidnuncs decided it wasn't any use,
The devil had let a thousand devils loose.

IV

Then folks began to read old books forbidden.
Carpenters orated and expatiated
On Orphic doctrines and wisdoms long hidden,
A Swede who couldn't speak began to talk Greek.
There were meetings in the park from dawn to dark.
And wild talk of razing the village, effacing
The plain little houses and the town replacing
With carved stone, columns and temples gracing
Gardens and vistas the water front embracing.
And others would create a brand new state.
So fire broke out in the strangest places.

SPRING LAKE

The belated traveler beheld elfin faces
Springing from nothing, to vanish in a second.
Potatoes unthrown went whizzing round corners.
Voices were heard and white fingers beckoned,
Till all the wise ones, doubters and scorners
Although they winced, in some way evinced
That their minds were convinced.
Something was wrong,
The evidence was strong,
The air was full of song:
You woke out of sleep and heard a violin,
A harp or a horn;
And rose up and followed the sound growing thin
At the break of morn.

v

Music, music, music was blown
Over the waters, out of the woodlands,
Grassy valleys and sunny meadow lands
In the mid spaces, tone on tone.
The pasturing flocks were sleeker grown
And multiplied in a way unknown. . . .
And little Alice bright of eye
Dreamed and began to prophesy:
And said the strayer, the cornet player,
Who took Starling Turner's wife away,
Is coming back at an early day:
Look out, said Alice, to Imogene,
Red-lipped, bright-eyed, turned eighteen,

STARVED ROCK

You have danced too much on the village green.
Look out for the cornet player, I mean.
I know who he is for my eyes are keen.
Your blood is desiring, but yet serene.
I know his face and his bright desire,
Laurel leaves are around his brow;
He carries a horn, but sometimes a lyre.
His eyes are blue and his face is fire.
Look out, said Alice, his touch is dire,
Keep to the house, or the church's spire.

VI

And what was next? The girl disappeared.
As Alice feared, no fate interfered.
A posse collected, hunted and peered,
Raced through the night till their eyes were bleared,
And looked for Imogene, cried and cheered
When a clew was found, or a doubt was cleared.
A posse with pitch-forks, scythes and axes,
Shot-guns, pistols, knives and rifles,
Hunts for Imogene, never relaxes,
Runs over meadows for luring trifles:
The wave of grain or a weed that tosses;
And curse and say what a terrible loss is
Come to Spring Lake: a wife's enticed,
And then this fairest maid is abducted.
Why are the innocent sacrificed?
We are a people well conducted.
What is the curse, or is it the war?

SPRING LAKE

Why is it every one here is housing
Fiddlers, idlers, fancy dancers.
At Milem Alkire's why carousing;
Everything that the good abhor
In lovers and romancers?
The world is mad, the village is mad,
Even the cattle bellow and run.
Old maid, young maid, man and lad
Have eaten of something half insane;
Such antics never before were done
And never it seems may be again
Under the shining sun.
And now comes villainy out of the fun.
Come with the torch, come with the halter,
Gather the posse, stay nor falter,
Catch the scoundrel who spoiled our peace
And hang him up in the maple tree's
Highest branch.   For what is the law
If it can't slip the noose and draw
This minstrel man to a thing of awe?

VII

Then the pastor said: Talk of the gallows
Is just the thing for it's righteous malice;
And we need hearts with piety callous
For work like this, I might say salus
Populi, but bright-eyed Alice
Can help us in this matter kinetic
Who has grown psychic and grown prophetic,

[133]

STARVED ROCK

Sees round corners, and looks through doors
And spies old treasure under the floors.
And I have heard that Alice averred,
The cornet player's the self-same bird
Who enticed the wife of Starling Turner
And kidnapped Imogene; he will spurn her
Later for some one else, unless we
Capture and hang the vile sojourner;
So now for Alice, he said, and bless me!

VIII

Alice came out to lead the mob
Catch the scoundrel and finish the job.
Down to Fruitport before it is dark
Come, said Alice, Joan of Arc.
Farmers, butchers, cobblers, dentists,
Lawyers, doctors, preachers, druggists
Hustled and ran in the afternoon,
Following Alice who led the way
Chanting an ancient roundelay,
A wild and haunting tune.
Her hair streamed over her little shoulders
Back in the wind for all beholders.
And her little feet were as swift and white
As waves that dance in the noonday light.
Youths were panting, middle aged men
Had to rest and resume again.
She ran the posse almost to death,
All were gasping and out of breath.

[134]

SPRING LAKE

At last they halted upon the ridge.
There! said Alice, beside the bridge
Under its shadow.   Look, he's there
Weaving lilies in Imogene's hair;
His musical instrument laid aside
Now he has charmed the maiden pride
Of Imogene who is not his bride,
Come, said Alice, before they hide.

IX

They ran from the ridge,
Looked under the bridge.
There! he escapes, said Alice, the fay.
Where?   Howled the mob! which is the way?
There's Imogene wrapped as if in a trance,
Said the preacher, there where the waters dance.
I saw as it were a shaft of light
Steal from her side, vanish from sight.
The cobbler said: it was like a comet;
The druggist, water by a bomb hit.
Yes, said the lawyer, I heard a splashing
And saw a light as of waters flashing
Or a thousand arrows of splendor flying
I heard a booming, banging, clanging
Of a bull's hide string, it was terrifying.
No, said Alice, this form of light,
That stole away and vanished from sight,
That was the fellow, said Alice, the sprite.

[135]

Go after him, follow through meadow and hollow
The God Apollo, the great Apollo!

x

They went to Imogene then and took her,
Spoke to her, slapped her hands and shook her,
Asked her who it was that forsook her,
Why she had left her home and wandered,
What was the dream she sat and pondered,
And Imogene said, it's a dream of dread,
Now that the glory of it is fled.
Where am I now, where is my lover?
God of my dreams, singer and rover.
I danced with the muses in flowering meadows;
We lay on lawns of whispering shadows;
We walked by moonlight where pine trees stood
Feathery clear in the crystal flood;
He gave me honey and grapes for food.
We rode on the clouds and counted the stars.
He sang me songs of the ancient wars.
He told me of cities and temples builded
Under his hand, we waded rivers
By star-light and by sun-light gilded;
By shades where the green of the laurel shivers.
But it came to this, and this I see:
Life is beautiful if you are free,
If you live yourself like the laurel tree.

SPRING LAKE

XI

Then some of them teased her, the posse seized her,
They tore the lilies out of her hair.
Back to the village, exclaimed the preacher,
Back to your home, exclaimed the teacher.
You've been befooled, said Alice, the fay,
And back went Imogene in despair,
Weeping all the way!

THE BARBER OF SEPO

Trimmed but not cut too short; the temples shaved,
Neck clipped around, not shaved, an oil shampoo,
You have a world of time before the train
And when it comes it stops ten minutes — then
The depot's just a block away.

                          Oh yes,
This is my own, my native town. But when
I earn the money to get out, I go.
I've had my share of bad luck — seems to me
Without my fault, as least life's actinism
Makes what we call our luck or lack of luck. . . .

Go down this street a block, find Burney Cole
And ask him why I was not graduated
From Sepo's High School at the time he was.
It was this way: I fell in love that spring
With Lillie Balzer, and it ended us,
Lillie and me, for finishing that year.
I thought of Lillie morning, noon and night
And Lillie thought of me, and so we flunked.
That thinned the class to Burney Cole, and he
Stood up and spoke twelve minutes scared to death.
Progress of Science was his theme, committed

THE BARBER OF SEPO

To memory, the gestures timed, they trained him
Out in the woods near Big Creek.

                                        Lil and I
Sat there and laughed — the town was in the hall,
Applause terrific, bouquets thick as hops.
And when they handed Burney his diploma
The crowd went wild.

                            How does this razor work?
Not shaving you too close? I try to please . . .
Burney was famous for a night, you see.
They thought his piece was wonderful, such command
Of language, depth of thought beyond his years.
Next morning with his ears and cheeks still burning,
Flushed like a god, as Keats says, Burney stood
Behind the counter in the grocery store
Beginning then to earn the means to take
A course in Science — when a customer
Came in and said: a piece of star tobacco,
Young fellow, hurry! Such is fame — one night
You're on a platform gathering in bouquets,
Next morning without honor and forgotten,
Commanded like a boot-black.

                                    Five years now
Burney has clerked, some say has given up
The course in science, and I hate to ask him . . .
But as for me, there was a lot of talk,
And Lillie went away, began to sport.
She's been around the world, is living now

STARVED ROCK

In Buenos Ayres. Love's a funny thing:
It levels ranks, puts monarch or savant
Beside the chorus girl and in her hands.
I stayed here, did not have to leave for shame,
But Lillie changed my life.

                              When she was gone
My conscience hurt me, and that very fall
When I was most susceptible, responsive,
And penitent, we had a great revival.
And just to use the lingo: after much
Wrestling at the Seat of Mercy, prayers
And ministrations then I saw the light,
Became converted, got the ecstasy.
I wrote to Lillie who was in Chicago
To seek salvation, told her of myself.
She wrote back, you are cracked — go take a pill. . . .
I know you've come to get your hair trimmed, shaved,
Also to hear my story — you shall hear.
The elders saw in me a likely man
And said there is a preacher. First I knew
They had a purse made up to send me off
To learn theology, and so I went.

I plunged into the stuff that preachers learn:
The Hebrew language, Aramaic and Syriac;
The Hebrew ideas — rapid survey — oh, yes,
Rapid survey, that was the usual thing.
Histories of Syria and Palestine;
Theology of the Synoptics, eschatology.

THE BARBER OF SEPO

Doctrine of the Trinity, Docetism,
And Christian writings to Eusebius.
Well, in the midst of all of this what happens?
A fellow shows me Draper and this stuff
Went up like shale and soft rock in a blast.
My room mate was John Smith, he handed me
This book of Draper's. What do you suppose?
This scamp was there to get at secret things,
Was laughing in his sleeve, had no belief.
He used to say: "They'd never know me now."
By which he meant he was a different person
In some round dozen places, and each place
Was different from the others, he was native
To each place, played his part there, was unknown
As fitted to another, hence his words
"They'd never know me now."

                And so it was
This John Smith acted through the course, came through
A finished preacher. But they found me out
As soon as Draper gnawed my faith in two.
The good folks back in Sepo took away
The purse they lent and left me high and dry.
So I came back and learned the barber's trade,
And here I am. But when I save enough
I mean to start a little magazine
To show what is the matter. Do you know?

It's something on the shelf — not booze or jam:
It's that old bible, precious family bible,

STARVED ROCK

That record of the Hebrew thought and life —
That book that takes a course of years to study,
Requires Aramaic, Hebrew, Greek and Coptic
And epigraphy, metaphysics, not
Because the book itself is rich in these
But just because when you would know a book
In every character and turn of phrase
And know what's back of it and went into it
You draw the learning of the world, that's all.
Take Plato, if you will, and study him
After this manner, you will travel far
In every land and realm.   But this is nothing.
The preachers are a handful to the world.
They eat this dead stuff like bacteria
That clean away decay.   The harm is here
Among the populace, the country, all
That makes for life as life.

                              See what I mean?
We have three thousand people in this town.
Say in this state there are a thousand towns,
And say in every town on every Sunday
In every year this book is taught and preached
To every human being from the time
It's five years old as long as it will stand
And let itself be taught — what have you done?
You have created, kept intact a body,
An audience and voting strength — for whom,
The reformer, the fanatic, non-conformist,
The man of principle who wants a law

THE BARBER OF SEPO

And those who, whether consciously or not,
Live in the illusion that there is an end,
A consummation, fifth act to this world,
Millennium, as they say; and at the last
When you get rid of sin (but they must say
What sin is) then the world will be at peace,
Life finished, perfect, nothing more to do
But tend to business and enjoy yourself
And die in peace, reach heaven.   Don't you see?
These people are deluded.   For this stuff
Called life is like a pan of bread you knead:
You push it down one place and up it puffs
In another place.   And so while they control
The stuff of life through Hebrew influence
Of duty, business, fear, asceticism
And yes, materialism, for it is that,
The dough escaped, puffs out, the best of it,
Its greater, part escapes us.   So I say
That bible taught in every village, hamlet
And all its precepts, curses, notables,
Preached fifty times a year creates the crowd
That runs the country at the bidding of
Your mediocrities, your little statesmen,
Your little editors and moralists.
And that's your culture, your American
Kultur. . . .

            I'll finish you with eggs, it's better
Than soap is for the hair.   You've lots of time.
I think I'll start my magazine next year.

STARVED ROCK

Step down this way — over the bowl, that's it —
A moment while I ring this money up.
As I was saying — is the water cold? —
Now back into the chair — as I was saying
That book upon the shelf has made our culture.
We must undo it. . .
Yes, your train is whistling — so long!

THEY'D NEVER KNOW ME NOW

Let's sit here very quiet, self-controlled,
Talk quietly, under this glorious tree,
The internes are too far away to hear.
They will stand there if we are calm.

                                        You look
Much better than you did.   And as for me,
Since I tried leaping from my window, I
Seem on the mend, sleep better, do not feel
So much like running, flying from the fears
As I did three weeks since.   Here is my tale:

My first step in this world was as a soldier,
Turned seventeen and off to free the Cubans.
I landed at Matanzas, served my time.
Oh Liberty!   Oh! struggles to make free
All peoples, everywhere!   And when I saw
The American republic move to strike
The chains of tyranny, I said: I die
For such a cause, or live to see it won —
How glorious!   My youthful mind was full
Of Byron, Shelley, Paine, and many more —
And when I saw my republic go to war,
Just as a good Samaritan, I said,

STARVED ROCK

This is my hour, I'm on the pinnacle,
Life is divine at last.

But on a sudden
A north wind froze my waters, caught my stars
To points of vision which before had been
Mixed in the fluent time.   We up and stole
The Philippines, spit on our sacred charter,
Turned all the thing to guts, until I heard
Their growl alone which I thought spirit voices
When we had warred for Cuba!   'Twas enough;
What was my country?   Just a mass of slickers
Talking philanthropy and five per cent,
A pious, blundering booby lodged at last
In a great cæcum mouthing Destiny.
God, with a leader just an actor-man,
Clean shaven, shifty, shallow, whored upon
By mercantilists and their butcher creed.
I mean McKinley, Hanna.   Write it down:
They barbarized our Grecian temple, placed
Cheap colored windows in its marble walls —
May history be their hell.

But as for me,
They talked of God so much, I said at last
I'll learn all they can teach concerning God.
This restless soldier spirit led me on,
And just because I sensed the faithless age,
Loveless and purposeless except for gold,
The adventurer in me began to crop.

[146]

THEY'D NEVER KNOW ME NOW

Oh yes, the Cuban business started me.
And so I went to college to prepare
For the ministry, as they thought, go through the course
Called theological, saying for the first:
" They'd never know me now."

                              I see at last
I am not one but many minds at once,
And many personalities.   As a boy
I took the color of the leaves or wall
Where I was resting, climbing.   If in truth
I lived three months with an uncle, then they said
You look just like your uncle.   When I worked
Under a lawyer's tutelage, they said:
How much your face resembles his.   I knew
My face and voice and gestures simulated
Those I admired or lived with.   But besides
I took a certain pleasure, impish, maybe,
In egging on, agreeing with, the souls
Whom I sought out; I used to tell my uncle,
A man of firmest piety, what I heard
Of blasphemy about the village, just
To hear him deprecate it, look with dark
And flashing eyes upon such sin, while I,
With serious face and earnest sympathy
With what he felt, was laughing in my sleeve.
Here is the germ then of my after life:
The faculty that harmonized my hue
Of spirit with the place, the person, while

STARVED ROCK

Something in me, perhaps supremest self,
Stood quite aloof and smiled.

                                    But, as I said,
When our Republic left its hill of vision,
Descended to the place of herding hogs,
This self of me, the adventurer, rose up
And led me forth to play with life, and first
To try theology, as I have said . . .
I was a wonder bred among the crew
Of quiet, gate-toothed, crook-nosed psychopaths,
The foul-breathed, thick-lipped onanists who filled
The seminary, stared at me to see
How I learned Sanscrit, could defend and rout
The atheistic speculations.   Well,
What I enjoyed most was to get a crowd
Of celibates and talk of chastity,
And get them in a glow, and say to them:
The mind is fortified by abstinence,
The spirit clarified and lifted up —
I got a thrill somehow.   But all the time
I knew a girl named Ella.   Oftentimes
Lying beside her I would shriek with laughter
And she would ask, what is the matter, John?
And I would say: I'm thinking of a song
I heard one time: " They'd never know me now."
And Ella said: If Dr. Simpson knew
That you were here with me, you'd take a fall
Out of the Seminary's second floor. . . .

THEY'D NEVER KNOW ME NOW

But I went through and didn't fall. And thought
This is a way to live, I'll preach awhile,
And see what comes. I took a church and preached,
Was known as Smith the eloquent, the earnest.
But all the time I heard a voice that said:
" They'd never know me now." When I came in
The Sunday School and little children flocked
About my knees and patient teachers looked
With white, pure faces at me, then that voice
" They'd never know me now " was in my ear. . . .

Well, to go on, a widow in my church
Young, beautiful and rich began to beat
Her wings around my flame, and on the Sunday
I preached about the rich young man, she came,
Invited me to dinner. We commenced,
Were married in six months. And to conserve
Her properties I studied law, at last
Was spending days with brokers, business men,
Began to tell her that my health was failing,
Saw doctors frequently to play the part.
And then she said: You must resign your charge,
Your health is breaking, dear. And I resigned
To spend the time in checking mortgages,
Collecting rents: —" They'd never know me now " . . .

We went the round of summer places, travel,
Saw Europe, China, India and the Isles.
Near Florence had a villa for a time,
Met people of all kinds, when I was forty

STARVED ROCK

I had a thousand selves, but if I had
A self in truth it was submerged or scrawled
Like a palimpsest all over and so lost.
I didn't know myself, was anything
To every one, and everything to all.
I felt the walking age come on me now:
A polar bear in a terrible rhythm swings
His body back and forth behind the bars,
And I would walk in restlessness or think
Of other skies and places, teased and stung
By memories of my other selves, by wonder
About what may be happening here or there;
What are they doing now?   What is she doing?
There were a dozen shes to wonder about,
And if you think of one you wish to see,
And dream she knows delight apart from you,
You simply thrill, the wings you lost revolve,
Like thumbs, vestigial stubs — but there you sit.
Thank God the aeroplane came on to help,
And wipe out distance, for you find at last
Distance is tragedy, terrifies the soul
With space which must be mastered by the soul.

And so I bought a hydroplane.   Perhaps
Would be upon my lawn at sun-down holding
These children on my knees, a lovely picture!
Then as a fish darts out of darkened water
Into a water sun-lit, there would come
A thought — we'll say of Alice — in two hours
I'd be upon her little sleeping porch

THEY'D NEVER KNOW ME NOW

Two hundred miles away, beneath the stars
Of middle summer, having killed that space,
And found the hour I wanted — hearing too
" They'd never know me now " sung in my ears.

And I remember when we were in Florence
My tribe had gone to Milan for some weeks,
And I was quite alone, too bored to live.
One listless afternoon who should come in?
My wife's friend Constance — but to tell the truth
More friend of mine than hers, for all my life
I seemed to have these secret understandings,
And was two persons to a twain who thought
They were the bond, whereas the bond existed
Between myself and one, and to the other
Was not so much as dreamed.

                              And Constance brought
A certain Countess with her.   In a glance
We two, the Countess and myself, beheld
A flame that joined our hands.   And in a week
The Countess took me on her yacht to Capri,
And round the Mediterranean.   No one knew,
Not Constance, nor my wife, for I returned
Before she came from Milan.

                    Oh that week!
That breeze that sung the port-holes, waters blue
And stars at night and music; and the Countess
Whose voice was like a lute of gold, who lived,

STARVED ROCK

Knew life, was unafraid. She heard me say
"They'd never know me now." And softly murmured
Smiling the while: il lupo cangia
Il pelo ma non il vizio
Adding, Qual matto! Something yet remains
That makes you charming! Oh the feasts and wine,
The songs and poems, till at last too soon
We anchored in the bay of Naples. When
I saw Vesuvius, then I felt again
That sinking of the heart that I had known,
That sickness, strange, nostalgia, from a boy,
Of which a word again. But now it was
Precursive of the end, the finished idyll.
The Countess took my hand, with misty eyes —
They let me off and rowed me to the dock,
I caught the train to Florence, magically
Before I had forgotten, seemed to be
Upon the yacht still, was in truth alone
Amid the silence of my dining room,
Supping alone — "They'd never know me now!"

Later I had the fever, was delirious
And saw myself receding as if backing
Into a funnel toward the little end,
And growing smaller as the funnel narrowed
Until I was so small I held myself
Within the palm's hand of my other self,
Laughed like a devil, scared the nurse to death,
Saying "They'd never know me now — just look!"
My wife too had the fever. I awoke

THEY'D NEVER KNOW ME NOW

Out of this illness, found that she was gone,
Had died a week before and for a week
Had been entombed while I was raving — then
If any real self of me ever was it came
Back to me then. I bowed my head and wept
And scanned my life back:

                    What was that in me
Which made me homesick from a boy right through
This life of mine, not for my home, for something,
Some place, some hand, some scene, which made me dread
All partings, overwhelmed me with a grief
For ended raptures, kept my brain too full
Of memories, never lost, that grew until
I lost myself, and seemed a thousand selves
Wandering through a thousand years, how restless!

Then mutterings shook our skies! Another war,
France, Germany and England, so it seemed
Best to return here to America.
I gathered up the children — all but one,
The boy eighteen escaped me, ran away
And joined the English army. Now I saw
One self of me repeated, that which went
To free the Cubans! Curse these freedom wars!
They shipped him off to India, soon he had
His fill of liberty. But I came back
And here I am. " They'd never know me now! "

[153]

STARVED ROCK

For what is left of me, what ever was
To be peeled off to realest core? The soldier
Gone out of me entirely; long ago,
The dreamer of a better world; the self
That said I'm on the pinnacle, took arms
To free the Cubans; self of me that hungered
For pyramids and mountains, ancient streams,
Nile and the Ganges; self of me that turned
To be a father holding on his knees
A romping bevy; self of me that dreamed
One heart, one hand enough, oh even the self
That dreamed there is a hand a heart for me,
Who found in truth no solace in the wife
But only a teasing, torturing recollection
That I had missed the one, or missed the many.

So I was in America again,
Had fled the war and plunged into the war: —
The waves roared yonder, but the shores were here
Where wreckage, putrid monsters were thrown up,
Corpses of ancient liberties and bones
Of treasured beauty; and I saw the Land
Don every despot weapon, as it did
When I fought for the Cubans, even worse.
They shipped my boy to Africa; in spite
Of censorship I pieced the picture out,
Knew what he suffered, how they took his faith
And dimmed its flame with ordure. Then came forth
That father self of me. I brooded on
His blue eyes, gentle ways, sat terrified

THEY'D NEVER KNOW ME NOW

And tried to trace the days through and the years
When he had slipped from just a little boy
Into a stripling, soldier finally —
While I — what was I doing? Oh, my God,
Living these other selves, oblivious
That this boy was. I'd jump from soundest sleep
Thinking of him in Africa, and seized
With dreams that I must fly to him. O years
Wherein I lost that boy. How could I live
So many lives and not lose out of some,
Some precious thing? Well, then I broke at last,
They brought me here: " They'd never know me now."

NEL MEZZO DEL CAMMIN

You call this a world! Cloud cuckoo town,
Nephelo coccygia, warp and woof,
Now at the last I write it down,
Since I no longer have the proof
To show it isn't opera bouffe,
A moving picture film and scene;
Stage world, with the glue between
The angels' feathers, the devil's hoof
Neither violent nor venene.

    *   *   *   *   *

Eheu! The middle of the way too —
Gethsemane and left in the lurch.
Storms frowning up the dying day too,
Bending a weed that was a birch.
I can step right over the tallest church.
Trumpets have shrunk to trumpet toys,
Tottle-te-toot! I hear the clocks
Ticking in paper breasts. What noise!
Gorges and towering rocks
Are just the canvas He employs,
With gelatine rivers and candy lochs,
Shored in with painted blocks.

I passed through a jungle where smoky mosses
Hung from the trees, the crocodile

[156]

NEL MEZZO DEL CAMMIN

Slept or clambered about the fosses;
Buzzards roosting, not very vile;
Rivers of red-ink shed for crosses.
Centaurs with arrows file on file
Drew and shouted: he seems to smile
Let's make him weep a while.

Look out for the lion! Said I, with a scowl,
Let the lion growl:
Cat-gut scraped in the painted wings.
Does the terrible tiger howl:
Tin cans and resined strings.
Do the dead gibber and does the owl
Hoot where the shroud is slipping, clings?
Who pressed the squeaky springs
In the death bird that it sings?

And you, sir! Well, one time I was sure
You carried a poisoned dart!
And now you're empty space as pure
As the sky when clouds are blown apart.
Ether! Radium! Nothing! A cure
For grit and dust which start
Grief in this Waterbury heart.

For I had trod the cobra, found
He is but calico, cotton stuffed.
The boa chased me round and round,
Hyenas tracked me, licked and snuffed,

STARVED ROCK

And made my poor heart flutter and pound,
Until I saw the mirror is all,
And the wood became a rare-bit dream
With monstrous faces and figures packed.
And then you ask: Is the mirror cracked,
Or is it so bright that it casts a beam
Through all the shadow scheme?

One time I saw a river's bank
Shaved down with spades as sheer as a wall,
Wasp holes, snake holes cut in two
Brought these molds of earth to view.
I turned away where the air was blank
And here was a thing fantastical:
Space was cored like the honey comb
With forms of things that crawl and roam,
Animals, men. As I am alive
I saw the form of a horse and cow
Edged with air and hollow as space.
But a horse and cow began to thrive
In just a second, a drifting mist
Flowed into the molds before my face.
And the animals moved, I don't know how,
Out of the all surrounding mesh,
Creatures of bone and flesh!

And it was just the same with men. I vow
I saw an astral stuff poured in
Pockets of air and men became
Voices talking of good and evil,

NEL MEZZO DEL CAMMIN

Virtue, courage, vice and sin,
God and the devil.

For the all unfolding Air is what?
The Great Idea, if so I may say,
A sort of Ocean leaping to waves.
And what do you care if they pass away?
They sink to their source, not into graves.
Beasts may vanish, races decay,
The Ocean will always remain the same;
With new waves rising, no two alike;
Waves that are little and waves that rise
In storms and touch the skies.

R. Browning, you were a man of power,
But I don't think much of your tower.
And I see no use of blowing a horn,
The tower is merely papier-maché,
And comes no higher than to my knees.
I step right over it — pick a flower,
Purple, it may be, called heart's ease
And go with the way of the seas.

For I am an optimist better than you:
This dream is hell, but it's all to the good:
The Ocean is water in calm or flood.
There's nothing wrecked, or wrongly wrought,
There's nothing real but Thought!

THE OAK TREE

The oak in later August,
Before his leaves are strewn,
And the sky is blue as June,
Trembles from trunk to branches
For frosts that will be soon
From the valleys of the moon!

For breezes blown in August
Veer north with cold and rain;
And the oak tree sighs and shivers
For lights that shift and wane:
As a strong man sees the specters
Of age, disease and pain,
The oak flings up to heaven
His branches in the rain.

September comes, September
Spreads out a sky that chills.
The owl hoots and the cricket
Beside the roadway shrills,
And on the stricken hills.
But the oak tree, the oak tree
Still flaunts his shining leaves.
No change has come but swallows
Who fled the summer eaves!

THE OAK TREE

But when October breezes,
And cold November gales
Descend upon the oak tree
What strength of him avails,
Grown naked to the tempest,
For life that sleeps and fails?
O oak tree, oak tree,
The winter snow prevails!
It cannot be your branches,
It is the wind that wails!

THE HOUSE ON THE HILL

Eagle, your broken wings are tangled
Among the mountain ferns
On a ledge of rock on high.
Below the yawning chasm turns
To blackness, but the evening planet burns
Above the gulf in a gold and purple sky!

Vultures and kites
Fly to their rookeries
In the rocks
With swift and ragged wings against the lights.
From levels and from leas
Haste the returning flocks.
Foxes have holes and serpents the grass for flight.
Eagle, arise! It is night.

The world's wanderer finds you
As he climbs the mountains
In the unending quest.
Can you spread wings across the darkening chasm
To the craggy nest,
Where the foreboding mate lies still?
Croak for the evening star,
And beat your shattered wings against your breast!
Across the gulf the wanderer sees afar
A light in the house on the hill!

That's right, sponge off his face. My name? Oh, yes,
James Frothingham, a reverend, have the church
At the corner of Ayer and Knox Streets, Methodist.
As I was passing by a vile saloon
Some men were entering the back room, saying
Is he dead or drunk, and such things. I looked in,
Went in at last and saw this fellow there,
Hunched, doubled down into a chair asleep,
Mud on his face as you saw, clothes bespattered,
The smell of drink upon him. Then we took him
And brought him here, I helped, a Christian duty.
But more important, if he wakes I'm here
To bring his soul to Christ before he dies —
And he is dying. Yes, it's plain enough
The snows of death are falling. Sponge his face,
And wash his hands! I never saw such hands
Slender and beautiful! Now you have sponged
His face, look at that brow — it terrifies —
He looks now like a god — who is this man?
I'll tell you all I know: These men were talking
And this is what they said: This is the fellow
They voted yesterday from booth to booth,
They voted him twenty times, and kept him drunk
To vote him. First they found him at the station,
A little tipsy, talking of his griefs.

STARVED ROCK

The conductor put him off here, being drunk.
And so these fellows for election day
Took him in hand and voted him around,
This was the talk.

                    Look at the curse of drink!
If he had touched no drink, he had not been
Tipsy to fall into these ruffian hands,
Who gave him drink and drink and used him thus
To violate the suffrage, lose his life
Through drink, as he will lose it.   He is dying,
Death comes of Sin — what plainer truth than this?
Sin blinds, too, for that brow could comprehend
All things by using what God gave to it.
I do not know his name, with your permission
I'll search his pockets — yes, here is a letter —
No signature, looks like a draught — I'll read:

" Why have you wounded me with words like these:
' He has great genius but no moral sense,'
And written to another!   Oh my love!
By this love which I bear you, by the God
Who reigns in heaven do I swear to you
My soul is like a wandering star, consumed
By its own passion, fire, and the eternal
Longing for the eternal, wandering, erring,
But flaming, loving light, aspiring to
The Light of Lights, some sun, I do not know.
It is incapable of aught but honor.
And save for follies, trifles in excess,

[164]

Which I lament, but which in men of wealth,
Or worldly power would never raise a word,
I can recall no act of mine to bring
A blush to your cheek or to mine.

                                My love,
My erring which has counted, by the test
Of strength or weakness for the game of life,
Has been Quixotic honor, chivalry.
And to indulge this feeling I have paid,
Though it has been my true voluptuousness,
My highest, purest pleasure. Yes, for this
I threw away a fortune, glad to throw it,
Rather than suffer wrong, though trivial,
As worldly men would count it: — for a father's
Laughter at my writing turned away
To follow voices, and defied his will
To harness me to business. So it is
To keep my spirit spotless from the world,
As I have visioned things, I came at last
By this deserted shore, alone, alone,
Now quite alone since you withdrew yourself,
Took back your hand and left me to my way,
Traveled so long that I can see the tomb
At the vista's end not very far.

                                Oh, love,
Why is there not a heart that loves but mine?
If you had been a Magdalen, I had pressed
Your head against my breast and kept you there —

But you — my spirit drifts with stricken wings —
But you because of gossip, crawling words
About my drinking, lies as I shall prove,
Can hold a handkerchief upon your eyes
To hide tumultuous tears, extend your hand
And say farewell forever, cut our lives
Of days or months, fragile and trivial
Asunder — when your hand, your faith, your love
Had cured me of my spirit's desolation,
My terror of this solitude in life —
Or if it cured me not, I had been eased,
And you had gained for giving — what have you
For your decision? Sorrow, if you love me,
Perhaps a conscience whisper that you failed
In justice, sacrifice; perhaps the thought
Life with me drinking, to the excess you thought,
Is better than a life where I am not.
What have you gained? In a few years we two
Will be at one with earth — before it comes
Are not sweet hours together worth the cost
Of a little drink? You who have riches, need not
My labors for your bread, but need my love,
Which you crush out. But as to drink, I swear
I do not drink."

                       Ahem! the fellow stirs
But will not wake, I fear. You heard that last:
He swears he does not drink. Drink and untruth
Go always hand in hand. This letter's long —
Let's see what he comes up with at the last:

WASHINGTON HOSPITAL

"But as to drink, I swear I do not drink —
How if I drank could I produce the works
I have produced? A giant's task, when drink
Sustains me not, is not my nutriment
As hock and soda water were for Byron,
But sets me flaming wild, a little drink
Will set me flaming, poisons me, I know.
And yet I must partake of drink sometimes
For life is flying, is recession, we
Are shrinking back into ourselves, at last
The arms we shrank from close about us — death's.
And there are souls born lonely; I am one.
And gifted with the glance of looking through
The shams, the opera bouffe, and I am one.
Often after a stretch of toil when I
Come out of the trance of writing spent and wracked,
I used to walk to High Bridge, sit and muse,
(For this brain never stops and that's my curse,)
Upon this monstrous world and why it is;
And why the souls who love the beautiful,
And love it only and are doomed to speak
Its wonder and its terror are alone,
Misunderstood and hunted, fouled by falsehood,
Have crumbs upon the steps, are licked by dogs,
Or else are starved. And why it is that I
Must go about, a beggar, with my songs
Exchanging them for bread. And then it is
When this poor brain like the creative stuff,
The central purpose, whirls, as I have written,
And will not stop — drink! for oblivion,

For rest, to get away from self, back faster
From the pursuing Nothing.

                    Yet, my love,
Think out what causes judgments, standards, tastes;
And why it was that Southey, Wordsworth won
The organic national praise and Shelley lost,
And Byron lost it — Southey the sycophant,
Wordsworth the dull adherent, renegade —
These two against these spirits who came here
To sing of Liberty — and look at me,
A wanderer and a poor, rejected man,
While usurers, slave owners rule the land,
And the cities reek with hypocrites, who step
On Freedom and on Beauty, are rewarded,
Praised, fed and honored for it. Then behold
Your friend who loves you, hunted, buffeted,
For a little drink, when in spite of drink and even
Because of drink, who knows? I have achieved,
Written these books. And what is life beside,
Whether with drink or whether with abstinence,
Except to sing your song and die, what course
Can stave the event, the wage of life, not sin?
Oh if you knew what love I have for you!
All of my powers are not enough to tell
How all my heart is yours, how I have found
Eternal things through you, cannot surrender
Your love, your heart, without I lose some life,
Some vital part of me — and yet farewell,
For you have willed it so, and I submit.

I rise up in my loneliness, seek the sun
To shine about me in my loneliness,
Submit and say farewell."

                     He spoke some words!
What was it that he said?   His head rolls over.
The man is dead!   What was it that he said?
Something about " no more " it seemed to me.
Whom shall we notify?   Go tell the police!
Here! wait, I overlooked some writing — yes,
A name is on this letter — why, look here,
It's EDGAR ALLAN POE! — I know that name —
He wrote a poem once about sleigh bells —
His brow looks whiter, bigger than it did.
Cover him with a sheet — I'll tell the police!

NEITHER FAITH NOR BEAUTY CAN REMAIN

Neither faith nor beauty can remain:
Change is our life from hour to hour,
Pain follows after pain,
As ruined flower lies down with ruined flower.

* * * * *

Now you are mine. But in a day to be
Beyond the seas, in cities strange and new
To-day will be a memory
Of a day ephemerally true.

* * * * *

Last night with cheek pressed close to cheek
Through the brief hours we slept.
It must be always so, I heard you speak,
Love found, forever must be kept.

* * * * *

But already we were changed, even as the day
Invisibly transforms its light.
We prayed together then for dawn's delay,
Praying, praying through the night.

* * * * *

Against the change which takes all loveliness,
The truth our desperate hearts would keep,

NEITHER FAITH NOR BEAUTY CAN REMAIN

The memory to be, when comfortless,
Save for the memory we shall yearn for sleep;

* * * * *

Against the sinking flame which no more lights
Our faces, neither any more desired
Through desireless days and nights,
And senses fast expiring and expired.

THE END

Printed in the United States of America.

[171]